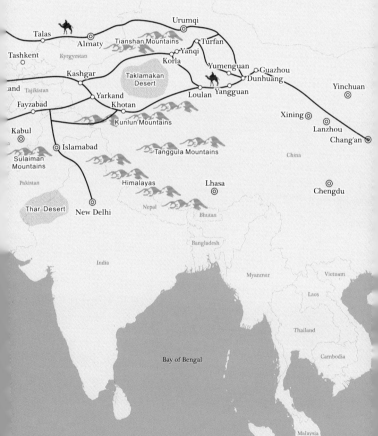

DUNHUANG

A City on the Silk Road

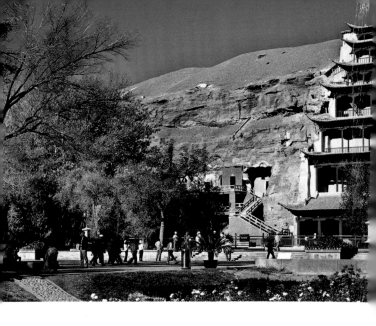

CONTENTS

Sights and Tours

Directory

1. MOGAO CAVES – SANWEI MOUNTAIN (P38)

When Northern Liang monks Le Zun and Fa Liang first cut into a cliff face by the Daquan River they could have no idea what they were beginning. Over the next 1000 years faithful artists would create more than 700 cave temples with 45, 000sqm of murals. Few places on Earth rival the sense of history these caves evoke. A hike around the nearby Sanwei Mountain offers a sense of perspective.

2. MOON CRESCENT SPRING AND MINGSHA HILL (P74)

Located just 6km south of Dunhuang city, and visible from downtown, Mingsha is less a hill and more a sea of mighty sand dunes. This is desert landscape of the imagination: golden sand dunes cascading towards the horizon. Except remarkably, the area is not entirely parched. A small oasis bubbles to the surface amongst the dunes.

3. WESTERN THOUSAND BUDDHA CAVES · YUMENGUAN · HAN GREAT WALL · YADAN (P80)

This route, heading southwest through the desert to Yumenguan, covers some of the greatest highlights that Dunhuang has to offer, from the hidden treasures of the Western Thousand Buddha Caves, to the poetic desiccation of the Jade Gate Pass and the Han Great Wall, and the eerie desert wilderness of Yadan.

4. YANGGUAN – GRAPE VALLEY (P98)
This excursion southwest through the desert takes in the one of the most enjoyable museums in China at the romantic Yangguan, site of another Han dynasty border gate, and offers an opportunity for bucolic relaxation in Yangguan's Grape Valley.

5. XUANQUANZHI POST STATION · SUOYANG RUINS · YULIN CAVES (P106)
En route to the Buddhist caves site of Yulin, visitors will pass through some stunningly bleak desert scenery as well as a spattering of verdant oasis towns. About forty minutes along the road from Dunhuang is the site of a Han Dynasty post station. If the journey onto Yulin proves fatiguing, in the surrounding desert are the well-preserved ruins of Suoyang.

6. AROUND DUNHUANG TOWN (P116)
2000 year old Dunhuang, one of four fabled frontier garrison towns, is devoid of the pollution and congestion that tarnishes many Chinese cityscapes today. The city offers a number of attractions including the lively Night Market, an artists' village and the excellent Dunhuang City Museum.

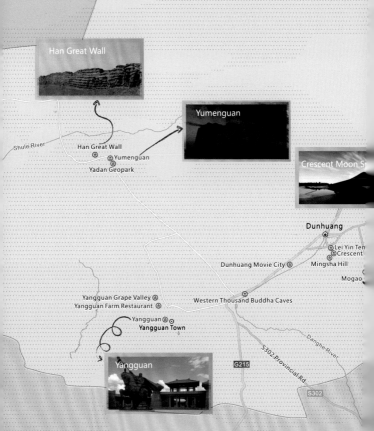

Dunhuang Region

Xinjiang Province

Han Great Wall

Yumenguan

Crescent Moon S

Shule River

Han Great Wall

Yumenguan

Yadan Geopark

Dunhuang

Lei Yin Ten
Crescent
Mingsha Hill

Dunhuang Movie City

Mogao

Yangguan Grape Valley
Yangguan Farm Restaurant

Western Thousand Buddha Caves

Yangguan
Yangguan Town

Danghe River

S302 Provincial Rd

Yangguan

G215

S302

Aksai Kazak Autonomous County

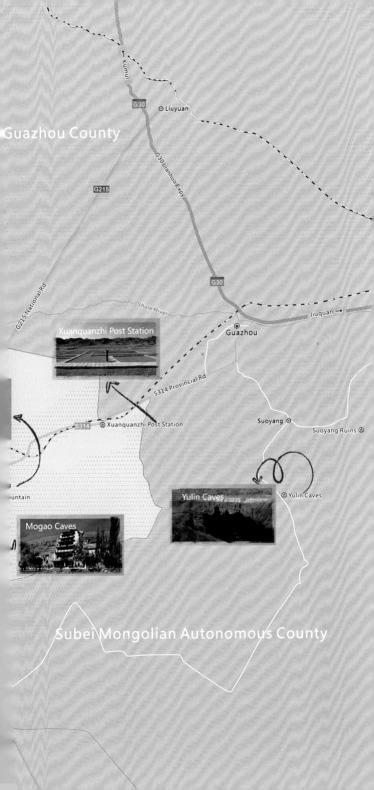

Guazhou County

Kumul ↑

G30

⊙ Liuyuan

G30 Lianhuo Expy

G215

G215 National Rd

Shule River

Jiuquan →

G30

Xuanquanzhi Post Station

⊙ Guazhou

S314 Provincial Rd

S314 ⊙ Xuanquanzhi Post Station

Suoyang ⊙

Suoyang Ruins ⊛

ountain

Yulin Caves

⊙ Yulin Caves

Mogao Caves

Subei Mongolian Autonomous County

© Dunhuang: A City on the Silk Road, Make-Do Publishing, 2015.
19th Floor, 262 Des Voeux Road Central, Hong Kong.
Writing: Thomas Bird, Harvey Thomlinson.
Photography: Li Zhengde.
Planning: Zhan Shunzhou, Jia Taibin.
Design: Mandy Wang.

Acknowledgements and thanks: Dunhuang Academy, Dunhuang Government, Lucy Guan, Dolly Huang, Zhang Pin, Zhang Qiujing.

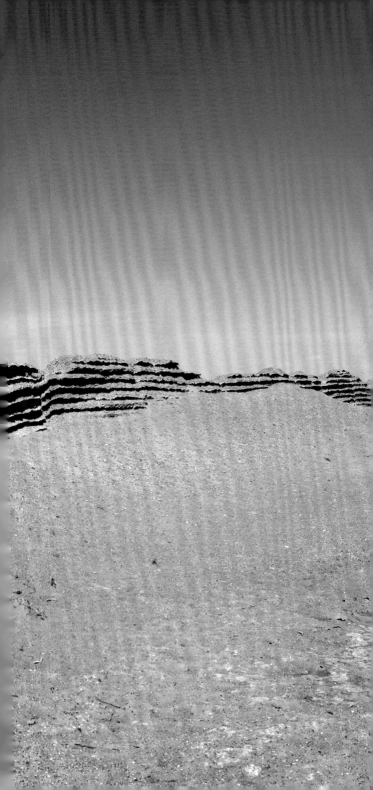

Introduction

For more than a millenium, Dunhuang on the ancient Silk Road was one of the ancient world's most important meeting places of East and West. This unique history is reflected in today's city which is again hosting a growing number of Silk Road explorers.

Dunhuang acquired its current name two thousand years ago during the Han dynasty. The new name–meaning Blazing Beacon–signified the settlement's upgraded status to that of imperial garrison town. After Emperor Wu of the Han sent envoys to Central Asia, trade exploded along what would become known as the Silk Road. Dunhuang offered the ideal locale for merchants to rest as they prepared for, or recovered from, the most gruelling leg of the ancient trade route. Its location on the Dang River, which fed the last fertile land before the great deserts of the Tarim basin, soon made it a bustling market town.

Especially before the development of the maritime Silk Road under the Song dynasty (960-1279,) Dunhuang was a unique confluence where Chinese, Indian, Greek and Islamic cultures met. As a strategic hub between the Chinese central plains and the Western regions, Dunhuang was a place where foreign ideas and inventions would first make landfall in China. These would include religious imports seeking to fill the spiritual vacuum left by Confucianism. First, the gentle Indian faith of Buddhism travelled to China via the Silk Road, and later, sword-wielding Islam took the Middle Kingdom by storm. Both would leave their indelible mark on Dunhuang.

Modern Dunhuang pilgrims are drawn above all by the incomparable art treasures of the Mogao Caves. It is these UNESCO protected heritage sites, the murals and statues housed in the Western Thousand Buddha

Caves, Yulin. Caves and most famously, the Mogao Caves, that underpin Dunhuang's emerging reputation as a cultural travel destination. In 1979, Dunhuang became the first city in China to be opened to the outside world and in 1992 it was approved as a tourism development zone. The city has identified 241 sites of cultural interest, including three UNESCO heritage sites (Mogao, Yumenguan and Xuanquanzhi,) six national level and nine provincial level attractions.

Visitors can roam the crumbling frontier of the Han empire of 2,000 years ago. The original Great Wall, begun during Qin Shihuang's reign, was extended to Dunhuang. Passes like Yumenguan were full of romantic resonance for centuries of Chinese poets. The remnants of the Han Great Wall, including 80 beacons and a military granary and border post, have been preserved by the dry climate and are now major sightseeing draws.

If its historical legacy isn't enough to get you booking your ticket, Dunhuang offers more for travellers in the surrounding desert. Whether you seek silence in the eerily crafted rock formations of the Dunhuang Yadan National Geopark, camel trekking across the Mingsha dunes, or fine wine in the surreal oasis village of Grape Valley, it is the diversity of the environment that strokes awe in visitors. Indeed, it is reasonable to say that the otherworldliness of the landscape, and the incorporeal art it has inspired, are inseparable. And it is the combination of geography and heritage that make this ancient border land a truly special place to visit, one that can only be experienced first-hand.

Cultural Legacy

Dunhuang's signifiance in the story of humanity lies in its position as a cosmopolitan focal point where the four major cultural systems of China, India, Greece and India met and collided. A unique culture, open, outward looking and cosmopolitan culture was forged whose legacy makes this city on the edge of the Gobi desert an important site for understanding the ancient world.

The Mogao Caves' murals are a priceless record of religious faith, dynastic history and everyday life which show an assimilation of cultures and artistic styles from both the Chinese Central Plains and Central Asia. During the peak of Mogao Cave art during the Tang (618-906) dynasty, great masterpieces like the Western Pure Land illustration on the south wall of Cave 220 were created. Meanwhle the 45,000 documents in Chinese, Tibetan and many other languages found in the Library Cave make Dunhuang a centre of international scholarship about ancient eastern cultures.

Dunhuang also offers an important window onto the mighty Han dynasty (206BCE-220CE.) No fewer than 82% of known document slips dating from this period were found preserved in the sands of the northwest of China, with Dunhuang accounting for the largest number of these. The more than 32,000 slips uncovered at the ancient post station of Xuanquanzhi include the earliest examples of paper with writing.

Visiting

The modest but pleasant prefecture level city of Dunhuang is where most latter day Silk Road pilgrims arrive by plane, train or bus. The city has welcomed travellers for millennia and offers a broad range of hotels and restaurants to suit most budgets. Local highlights include the Night Market and fine museums. Five kilometres out of town, the Crescent Moon Lake is a poetic symbol of Dunhuang. It is possible to bed down here at the foot of the Mingsha dunes. The Mogao Caves are located half an hour from downtown Dunhuang. A tour of the caves can be augmented by a visit to the digital centre or a hike around Sanwei Mountain. Meanwhile other sites including the Han Great Wall and Yadan National Geopark are scattered around the desert within a 180km (one to two hours' drive) radius of Dunhuang. Dunhuang's tourism infrastructure is still under development meaning that visitors to this remote place should improvise to get the most out of their experience.

Itineraries

Six chapters of this book suggest itineraries that can be adapted to suit all budgets, interests and trip lengths. Details about getting around, where to stay and how much to budget for can all be found in Practical Information. One week should be a fairly comfortable period in which to experience most of the region's attractions. Those with more time for could extend their Dunhung sojourn with camel hikes and camping.

Geography

Gansu is one of China's most unusual shaped provinces. It is long and narrow, with two bulbous extremities and it appears to arc around neighbouring Qinghai. This distinctive form has been shaped by the dramatic geography of the region. Gansu is wedged between the two elevated plains, the Tibetan Plateau to the west and Loess Plateau to the east. The south of the province, which the Yellow River flows through, is generally mountainous whereas the north is far flatter. The vast majority of this landlocked territory rests over 1000 metres above sea level. The Hexi Corridor, a natural land passage and ancient trade route, runs for a thousand kilometres from the provincial capital Lanzhou in the south to the Jade Gate near Dunhuang.

Dunhuang is a located at the northwest of the province, geographically closer to Xinjiang than the administrative centre in Lanzhou. Indeed, as the last town on the Hexi Corridor, it appears to look towards Xinjiang, an ethnically diverse, semiautonomous region, whose name means New Frontier.

The city of 31,200km² is fed by the Dang River, which originates in the Shule South Mountains in Qinghai Province. The Dang is a vital lifeline making Dunhuang habitable in a largely inhospitable region. The city lies in a 1,400km oasis and is lined by sand-tolerant vegetation. Much of the city limits is given over to the cultivation of arable crops such as grapes, dates, apricots and melons, giving Dunhuang cause to be known as a 'fruit city.'

As one might expect of a desert, people don't come to Dunhuang for the flora and fauna. However, there are a few animals to watch out for including rare wild camels and a strange desert pheasant that makes its nest in the rocky landscape and prefers running to flight.

Landscape and Environment

The Gobi Desert, Asia's largest, is so big the Chinese often simply refer to it as the Endless Sea. As an oasis town, Dunhuang appears like a lonesome green island amidst this arid expanse. But the desert is anything but dull. In fact, the Gobi Desert is so diverse; it is broken-up into different areas depending on regional climate variation and topology.

South of Dunhuang are the rolling dunes that tend to epitomise desert land for many people. Driving between sights located outside of Dunhuang one passes plains of gravel that stretch to the horizon. Around Sanwei Hill the landscape is rocky, defined by boulders and craggy hillsides. The most spectacular terrain can be found in Dunhuang Yadan National Park where wind and sand erosion has carved bedrock hills into mysterious, often fantastic formations.

Dunhuang administers 31, 300km² of mostly desert land but 1, 400km² is fertile and green. Scattered about the desert are several small oasis towns. Fed by distant mountain rivers or groundwater, these verdant quarters, notably Grape Valley near Yang Guan, can appear quite surreal when compared with the abounding wilderness.

Environmentally speaking, the People's Republic is synonymous with smog these days. However, several factors have colluded to make Dunhuang's air breathable and clear: It is far from the coast, where much of the industrial build-up has occurred. It occupies a relatively isolated location in the Northwest, making large-scale manufacturing impractical. A principle industry is tourism, mandating a well-protected environment to ensure the tourist dollars keep rolling in. Dust, however, remains a problem as Dunhuang is bashed by desert winds and gets very little rain. Dunhuang occupies an extremely water poor region and this deficit is compounded by the rise in population that has accompanied the tourist boom.

When to Visit

If you're a sun lover you're in luck. Dunhuang receives 3,258 hours of bright sunshine annually, making it one of the sunniest cities in China. However, all that sunshine doesn't necessarily equate to warmth. During winter months, temperatures drop well into the minuses. January is the coldest month with an average of –8.3°C. Temperatures soar the in summer, reaching their highest during July, when daytime temperatures generally peak at well over 30°C. Precipitation is low and Dunhuang seldom sees rainfall. Summer months are likely to experience a few days of drizzle, which quickly evaporates. Around March and April, as the wind picks-up, Dunhuang is often subjected to sandstorms. The most comfortable times to visit are in late Spring and Autumn when you can enjoy Dunhuang without the searing summer heat, or the crowds that accompany the holiday season. The local authorities like to sing the praises of Dunhuang as a destination for all seasons. Winter is the low season, and certain places closedown for a period. However there are compensations such as the chance to see the Mogao Caves and Mingsha dunes under snow.

Population

The majority Han Chinese account for 90% of Dunhuang's population with the remaining 10% made-up by the Hui minority as well as smaller groups such as Tibetans, Kazaks, Mongolians, Miao, Manchu. The Han are of the northwestern ilk, independent wheat-eaters, toughed by eons subsisting in an unforgiving corner of North China. The Hui are one of China's most rootless ethnic groups, as they don't have a common language or homeland. The ten million or so Hui can be found distributed widely across China's Central Plains and the Northwest and find commonality in Islam,

which engenders many distinctive cultural characteristics, notably Hui cuisine.

Language and Culture

The people of Dunhuang speak Dunhuanghua, a sub-dialect relating to the provincial dialect Gansuhua, of which the capital city's Lanzhouhua is the most widely understood. All could be said to belong to Lanyin Mandarin, a version of the national tongue prevalent throughout the northeastern provinces of Gansu and Ningxia. Standard (Beijing) Mandarin is widely spoken and understood by all but a few elderly people and remote rural dwellers. As is commonplace across China, English is mandatory at school. That said, don't expect everyday people you meet to have much grasp of the language.

Islam is the first religion you're likely to encounter as the Hui Chinese dominate the local food and beverage industry. Most tourists gravitate to the outdoor Food Street near the Dunhuang Mosque after dark to feast on skewers of halal lamb and beef, or to devour bowls of Lanzhou Pulled Beef Noodles.

Buddhism, however, got there first and though its impact is less evident in the attire and eating habits of locals, it is Buddhism's legacy that is Dunhuang's principle attraction.

Economy

All sectors of Dunhuang's economy combined, the city garnered more than 10 billion yuan in 2013, of which tourism earnings of 48 billion accounted for nearly half. The economy is dependant to a large extent on service industries such as tourism, with agriculture relegated to scattered oases. Industry is decidedly low-key in Dunhuang, which is far away from China's thriving ports. The city is a prosperous town by north-west Chinese standards with all amenities you might require, including hospitals, schools, supermarkets, as well as bus, rail and air links.

History

Dunhuang's history is inextricably tied to the rhythm of interactions between the Chinese empire and nomads of the Western regions. There is evidence of human habitation in this area as early as 2000BCE. By the second century BCE, as the Han Dynasty tried to impose its control on the Western Regions, they met resistance from the Xiongnu tribes that then reigned supreme.

For the Chinese, Dunhuang's history starts with the expeditions of the great Han diplomat and explorer Zhang Qian (200-114BCE) who was dispatched by the Han Wu emperor on a perilous mission to the unknown lands beyond western borders of Han. He was captured by the Xiongnu for ten years before escaping back to Chang'an.

Emperor Wu wanted to establish commercial relations with semi-legendary Western territories like those of the Yuezhi, Dayuan, Kucha and others. After the failure of Zhang Qian's expedition to develop these ties, up to ten Chinese caravans a year were sent West towards Central and Western Asia, the largest of them numbering hundreds of people. These were eventually responsible for opening up the Western Silk Road.

Chinese capture Dunhuang

In 121BCE, 20 year old Hangeneral Huo Qubing wrote his name into history by leading 10,000 cavalry through the Hexi corridor. His two expeditions against the Xiongnu resulted in the capture of 30,000 Xiongnu soldiers and the assimilation of Dunhuang into the Han empire.

To consolidate the famous Han victory, in 112BCE four frontier garrison towns were set up in the region, including one at Dunhuang, to protect the Han against the still insurgent Xiongnu. Dunhuang was made part of Jiuwan prefecture, which records show at the time of establishment had 38,335 people and 11,006 families. The Han extended the Great Wall to Dunhuang and built a line of fortified beacon towns that stretched through the desert. The impressive Han postal system was extended here with a number of local post stations. Meanwhile, to bolster defence and expand cultivation, the Han encouraged settlement—

often of convicts sentenced to death—from the central China plains to Dunhuang, By the end of the Western Han dynasty in the second century CE, the population had soared to 280,000 and Dunhuang's walls were a symbol of safety and comfort for the flow of caravans that passed though the city .

For a time the Han even acquired control of the Tarim Basin region, thanks to the exploits of the great Eastern Han general Ban Chao (32-102CE,) who led campaigns against the Xiaognu and was awarded the title Protector General of the Western Regions. However this marked the furthest reach of Han control of territories west of Dunhuang and following his death the Xiongnu power waxed again.

Religion and Trade

Far from the great centres of Chinese power in Luoyang and later Chang'an, Dunhuang became a mingling point for peoples of East and West and a place where the foreign religions of Buddhism, Nestorianism and Islam could all be found. In the fourth century CE, the Mogao Caves near Dunhuang were founded by a roaming monk named Le Zen. This was more than a century before Buddhism was officially recognized by the Chinese state as a religion in 444. By the time of the Northern Liang a small community of monks had formed at the site. The ruling families of the Northern Wei and Northern Zhou dynasties built many caves here and by the Tang dynasty there were more than 1000 caves. Briefly, from 400 to 405 during the time of the Sixteen Kingdoms, Dunhuang was even a capital after Li Gao established the Western Liang here. In 405 the capital was moved from Dunhuang to Jiuquan and in 421 the Western Liang was conquered by the Northern Liang.

During the Sui dynasty Duhuang rose to a new period of greatness. With a reduction of the Turkish threat in the northwest, the Silk Road was open for business again, meaning a prodigious stream of merchants through Dunhuang. The Sui dynasty strengthened control of the Hexi corridor and placed a priority on strengthening trade with the Western regions. In 609 Emperor Yandi led a huge delegation from Chang'an to Zhanghe in the Hexi corridor for what became known as the Exposition of 10,000 Kingdoms. This event has been described as the earliest world trade convention as emissaries of over 27 kingdoms of the western regions came to pay homage.

The Silk Road

It was the German explorer Baron Ferdinard von Richthofen who coined the term "Silk Road." It's a name that's proved popular and enduring. It is, however, misleading as it implies one product travelling down one pathway in one direction. Caravans came from the West bearing gold, ivory, precious stones and glass, while those going West were laden with not just silk but other treasures such as ceramics and jade. It was along the Silk Road's 4,000 miles of interconnecting trade routes that technology, philosophy and religion travelled alongside the luxury goods of the ancient world. For over a thousand years, this patch work of trails traversed the most inhospitable regions on earth, connecting the empires of the Orient with those in the West. The iconic camel-trains, some numbering over a hundred beasts, not only endured the worst nature could throw at them as they negotiated such deserts as the dreaded Takimakan. Traders also confronted bandits and warring tribes in the barren lands of Central Asia where civilisation had only a tenuous hold.

Dunhuang: The "Throat" of the Silk Road

Dunhuang was a key staging post on the Silk Road that offered westbound traders an unenviable choice of two often deadly routes across the Gobi desert. The northern way passed through Yumenguan (the Jade Gate Pass) and crossed the neck of the Gobi through the oases of Turfan and Kuqa to Kashar at the foot of the Parmirs. The southern route went through Yangguan (the Sun Pass) and skirted the southern edges of the desert via Ketian (Khotan) and Shache (Yarkand) before turning north again to meet the other route at Kashgar. Dunhuang as it exercised control both the Yumenguan and Yangguan passes was therefore the "throat" of the Silk Road and one of its most important hubs.

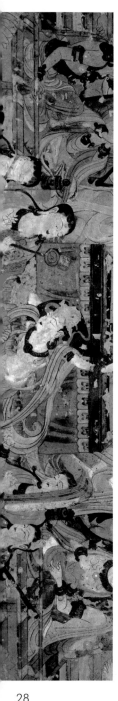

Tang Dynasty

By the time of Dunhuang's Tang dynasty zenith, the markets of the city overflowed with silk and porcelain from China's central plains, jade and jewelry from the Western regions and camels and horses from the north as well as local produce. The Silk Road city also benefited in the High Tang period from developments in the local economy and the establishment of an irrigation system of three rivers, one hundred canals, eight springs, and ten ponds: together with branches of the Dang River, this added up to over 700 li.

The 13 villages that made up Dunhuang were inhabited by people of Han, Tibetan, Persian, Hui and Korean descent with a mix of customs and religions such as Confucianism, Buddhism, Taoism, Machicheism, Zoroastrainism and Nestorianism. Dunhuang was also a hotbed of learning with a large number of local authority founded schools as well as those supported by monasteries.

The Tang era is regarded as the peak of artistic production at Mogao, with more than 70 caves dating from this time. Remarkable advances in narrative painting, in perspective and in lifelike sculpture were made, and artworks show the influence of the great Tang court at Chang'an, as well as of the Silk Road. The growing numbers of geometric designs that feature in the cave murals demonstrate western inspiration.

From 790 to 851, Dunhuang came under the influence of the Tibetans, who conquered the city in 781 after 11 years of resistance. During this period the first Tantric themes appear in the Mogao caves. In 848 Zhang Yichao led the people of Dunhuang to rise up against the Tibetan empire (Tufan) and recover Dunhuang and nearby regions from Tibetan rule. Dunhuang was again a Tang territory.

The End of the Silk Road

Dunhuang continued to be a target for incursions. In 1068 the city came under the rule of the Tanguts who founded the Western Xia dynasty. A prior Tangut incursion in 1036 is associated by historians with the decision by the Mogao monks to seal 45,000 manuscripts in a cave, where they were discovered in 1900 by the Taoist Abbot Wang. Although dispersed, this fabulous collection is an essential source for Asian history.

In 1227, Dunhuang was conquered again by the Mongols who destroyed much of it, but the rebuilt town became part of China again when Kublai Khan conquered the rest of China and founded the Yuan Dynasty.

It was during the Yuan dynasty that the Silk Road was finally superseded by seafaring traders manning bulky cargo ships. These grand new vessels could carry more in their hull than a hundred camels and the shipping lanes were anyone's to navigate, eliminating the tariffs paid to middlemen who controlled tapered passes. The Silk Road was officially abandoned during the Ming Dynasty.

By the 1890s the once thriving oasis town of Dunhuang had plunged into obscurity becoming little more than a thinly populated, dusty backwater but one that was on the brink of rediscovery by Silk Road adventurers like Aurel Stein and Paul Pelliot.

The Art of Mogao

Architecture

Three main types of cave were built at Mogao:

Meditation Caves: The square or rectangular design of the earliest caves was modelled on the Vihara (monk's residences) style of Indian Buddhist grottos such as Ajanta. The square stupa has small meditation cells along the niche and worshippers would circumnavigate the stupa to express devotion. Today only three examples of this type of cave remain at Dunhuang.

Central Pillared Caves: Popular up until the Northern Zhou (557-581) period, Central Pillared Caves were also inspired by a type of Indian architecture, the Chaitya. The rectangular main chamber contains a central square pillar with niches on either side of it, a gable ceiling at the front part and a flat ceiling at the back. However the gable ceiling imitates a Chinese-style traditional wooden structure.

Assembly Halls: Built mainly as places of worship for devout Buddhists, Assembly Halls became popular from the Tang Dynasty (618-907) and account for the largest number of caves in Dunhuang. The caves are usually square or rectangular with a main niche and one or more statues on an altar or in a niche.

Murals

For the monks of Mogao, visual art was very helpful in propagating religious doctrine. Sutra depictions and narratives of scenes from the Buddha's life occur prominently in the cave murals but there are also historical scenes, decorative images and donor images.

To make the murals, three layers of plaster were applied to a smooth wall surface on which to paint. The murals capture many moments of technical innovation in Chinese art. Some of the early caves like Cave 275 preserve the only surviving Chinese examples of a shading technique called Yunran which was imported from India. The technique, similar to the European Chiaroscuro style, used contrasts of light and dark to create a three-dimensional effect.

One great achievement is the evolution of complex narrative painting, which began in the Western Wei. Early paintings were generally flat with no three dimensional effect. From the Northern Wei the pattern shifts to a Chinese style reminiscent of scroll painting with scenes in horizontal rows. Paintings such as the 87 scenes of the life of Sakyamuni in Cave 290 contain fascinating detail of contemporary life including farming and an archery competition. The peak of large narrative paintings at Mogao was during the mighty Tang dynasty. This period also saw the development of the mature landscape drawing called Boneless 'meigu' which has no outlines. Mountains are often used for separating the episodes but in paintings such as that in Cave 323 are also part of the story. Other Tang Mogao treasures include the blue-green eight century landscape painting in Cave 103, a rare example of a style that was famous in Tang times but then lost.

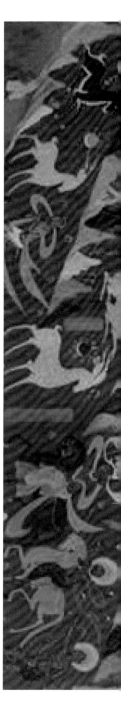

Important Subjects of the Murals

Characters

Sakyamuni.

Gautama Buddha, also known as Sakyamuni (Shakyamunni,) or Siddhārtha Gautama, was the founder of Buddhism. Popular scenes of Sakyamuni's life story that are the subject of murals in the caves include:

· *The Conception, in which the Buddha-to-be is riding an elephant descending to Earth;*

· *The Great Departure, in which Prince Sidhartha is riding on a horse in search of the meaning of life; and The Enlightenment, which was the first step of the Prince's search for enlightenment.*

· *The Defeat of Mara (see Cave 254) in which Sakyamuni is attacked by Mara (the king of demons) and three beautiful daughters who represent illusions…*

Cave 61 contains a mural illustrating the whole life of Sakyamuni.

Past Lives

Sakyamuni's previous lives (Jakata) are also a theme of the Mogao murals. There are more than 500 known Jakata tales in Buddhism, each representing one of the Buddha's previous lives. The most popular include:

· *Deer King Ruru forgiving the betrayal of a man he saved from drowning.*

· *Prince Mahasattva offering his body to feed a starving tigress and her cubs*

· *King Sivi offering his flesh to save a dove*

· *Prince Sudana renouncing all his belongings, including his own children*

These stories all emphasise Sakyamuni's good deeds and self-sacrifice in his previous lives and reveal the law of karma.

Avalokitesvara

Avalokitesvara, the Boddhisatva of infinite compassion, became especially popular in China where he was known as Guanyin, and in later caves he is sometimes a theme for an entire wall. Guanyin is usually portrayed with lavish clothes and jewelry and from the Tang era he increasingly has female characteristics.

Manjusri

Manjusri, Bodhisattva of Transcendental Wisdom, is known in China as Wenshu and for the Chinese is associated with the sacred mountain of Wutai in Shanxi.

Samantabhadra

The patron of the Lotus Sutra, Samantabhadra is credited with making the ten great vows which are the basis of a Bodhisattva. Together with Sakyamuni, the Bodhisattas Samantabhadra and Manjusri form the Sakyamuni Trinity in Buddhism. In China, Samantabhadra become associated with action, while Manjusri was associated with wisdom. Samantabhadra and Manjusri often appear in the murals as a pair.

Maitreya

The Boddhisatva Maitreya is regarded as a future Buddha who will appear on earth, achieve enlightenment and teach the dharma. In China, the Chinese monk Budai was claimed to be an incarnation of Baitreya and his depiction as a pot bellied Laughing Buddha became very popular throughout East Asia.

Bhaisaiyaguru.

Commonly referred to as the Medicine Buddha, Bhaisajyaguru is the Buddha of healing and medicine. On attaining Buddhahood he became the Buddha of the Eastern Pure Land. He is often depicted wearing a monk's robes and holding a jar of medicine nectar in his left hand and his right hand resting on his knee.

Sutras

Many of the Mogao murals illustrate the teachings of the Buddha. The following are some of the most commonly encountered sutras.

Lotus Sutra

One of the most popular and influential Buddhist texts, the Lotus Sutra presents itself as a discourse delivered by the Buddha late in his life. The Sutra was originally translated from Sanskrit into Chinese by Dharmaraksa in 286CE in Chang'an. The sutra uses parables to instruct on the attainment of Buddhist wisdom and was one of the first to introduce the term Mahayana or 'Great Vehicle' Buddhism.

Virmalakirti Sutra

The Virmalakirti Sutra contains a report of a teaching addressed to both Arhats and Bodhisattvas by a lay practitioner Vimalakirti, which culminates in the wordless teaching of silence. Vimalakirti feigns illness and when the ruler of the region and various officials visit him, he takes the opportunity to expound Dharma teachings.

Mahaparinirana Sutra

This sutra concerns the end of the Gautama Buddha's life and the focus of its teachings is the Buddha-nature and the possibility for all sentient beings to attain Buddhahod. The sutra was very influential in East Asian Buddhism.

Amitayus Sutra

Amitayus Sutra is one of the three major Buddhist sutras found within the Pure Land branch of Mahayana Buddhism. Amitayus is another name for the Buddha Amitabha, the main figure in Pure Land Buddhism, and this sutra focuses mainly on meditations and complex visualisation.

Sculpture

In earlier dynasties the backs of the main statues were attached to the wall, with their heads being made separately and then put on top of their bodies. Figures of Boddhisattvas, Apsaras and Thousand Buddha motifs are often in bas-relief and attached to the walls

In the Tang period we see fully detached statues for the first time. In contrast to the statues of early dynasties that are attached to the walls, the fully detachable statues could be admired from all sides. It was during the Tang perod however that two giant Buddha statues were constructed at the site, the largest one in 695 following an edict by Tang Empress Wu Zetian to build giant statues across the country. The two giant Buddhas are seen as reflecting the strength and self-confidence of the empire at this time. There are 2,415 statues remaining in Dunhuang, although many are Qing dynasty renovations.

1 Mogao Caves

Mogao might be regarded as an illustrated history of a millennium of the Silk Road and through the legacy of its murals and sculptures we can see the influence that Tibet, India and Central Asia had on China. Few places on Earth rival the sense of history these caves evoke.

Mogao Caves
(莫高窟 Mògāo Kū)

Location

When Northern Liang Monks Le Zun and Fa Liang first cut into a cliff face by the Daquan River they could have no idea what they were beginning. Over 1000 years, devout artists would create more than 700 cave temples with 45, 000m² of murals. The Mogao Caves are located 25 kilometres from town and line a cliff face, which is 1, 600 metres in length running from north to south. In the desert opposite stand Mongolian stupas, while in the distance one can make out the craggy outline of Sanwei Mountain. The grottos are divided simply into the southern section and northern section. The southern section contains 492 decorated temple caves whereas the northern section, containing 243 caves, is largely in a state of ruin.

It is possible to visit the Mogao Caves and Digital Centre either as part of a tour group or independently. A green city bus takes forty minutes from downtown and picks at the train station and at Charley Johng's hostel and The Silk Road Hotel downtown (RMB8.) Meanwhile a taxi costs about RMB40 from downtown.

Visiting Mogao

Due to conservation issues, it is only possible to visit the caves as part of a group with a tour guide appointed by the Dunhuang Academy. English tours are at 9am, 12pm and 2pm daily. Each tour lasts about two hours and takes in around eight to ten caves spanning a representative range of styles from different dynasties. Admission to the caves as part of a tour group costs RMB160/person, with a RMB20 surcharge for English guide services.

Digital Centre

To enhance the Mogao experience, the Dunhuang Academy encourages visitors to attend a screening of two short films at the Digital Centre established near the caves. The first film is a high octane, glossy drama depicting life in the ancient garrison town. The second is a spectacular visual experience that takes two to three thousand high-definition images of the murals in each cave and merges them into a 3D film. Simultaneous translation of both soundtracks is available via freely distributed headphones. This stereoscopic experience enables visitors to enjoy areas of the caves usually off limits to the public. Admission to the Digital Centre, including both films, is RMB60/person, which is additional to the cost of admission to the Mogao Caves.

After exiting the second film, visitors board buses for the short ride onto the caves site where you can sign up for the next available tour group. Being a premier tourist spot there are all the facilities one might expect at the entrance: restaurant, souvenir shop, car park and museum.

Dunhuang Stone Grotto Research Centre

Dunhuang Stone Grotto Research Centre affords a deeper and broader telling of the Dunhuang story. The museum comprises of three exhibition halls and an auditorium where films about Mogao art are screened. The first exhibition hall contains eight replica caves, each representing its particular era, from the Sixteen Kingdoms through the Yuan. The second hall tells the story of how the grottos were originally furnished, explaining the division of labour between the *lianggang* (excellent workmen) and the *qiaojian* (skilled workers) and the materials used to decorate Mogao's caves, such as animal glues and mineral pigment paint. One also learns of the vital financial role played by local patrons, including notable politicians, generals and soldiers. Treasures on display here include mural replicas, ancient silks, and manuscripts found in the Library Cave. A few articles testify to the Silk Road's influence including Persian silver coins and Christian scripture. There are Tang dice made of bone on display in addition to a host of textiles, leather clothes and animal bones, suggesting not all Buddhists were practising vegetarians!

The Story of Mogao

Origins

Legend tells of an itinerant Buddhist monk Le Zun, who one night in AD366 had a vision of thousands of Buddhas shining in the sky above Mingsha Hill. Taking this as divine inspiration, he cut a temple with a golden statue of the Buddha into the river cliff. Later another Buddhist Monk, Fa Liang, visiting Dunhuang, built a second cave and within a few decades about 70 grottos had been carved at Mogao.

From 366 until 1368, the history of cave creation at Mogao spans more than 1000 years and 11 dynasties. The evolution of the caves reflects the vagaries of dynastic history and influences from both the Chinese central plains and the Western Regions. Many earlier caves were renovated during later dynasties. By the High Tang, regarded by many as Mogao's artistic apogee, we see caves adorned with works of immaculate sophistication, enhanced by vignettes of life in capital Chang'an.

Early Caves

The first caves at Mogao such as the Northern Wei cave 254, with its square central stupas and niche sculptures look like Indian rock grottos. The relatively simple groups of niche statues typically feature a trio of Buddha and two disciples. Not until the Northern Zhou era (557 – 581) did larger group of main statues start to appear, with a group of five being common. The murals of these early caves also show a strong Indian influence.

It was during the Northern Wei dynasty (386 – 535) that a distinctive Dunhuang style first began to appear. Buddha images during the Western Wei (535 – 556) wear Chinese style clothes. Meanwhile Buddhas from the Northern Zhou era have a northern Chinese look of big heads and shoulders and short legs. The style and composition of the murals and the costumes worn by the carved figures also suggest exotic influences from lands along the Silk Road.

Dunhuang was profoundly affected by the Sui emperors' use of Buddhism as an instrument of government (581CE-618CE). Imperial patronage can be seen in the luxuriant imagery as well as in the accelerated speed of cave construction under the Sui. Several Sui era caves are extremely well preserved and contain magnificent murals such as the preaching scene in Cave 419.

Apsaras

The evolution of Dunhuang art can be seen in the depictions of Apsaras, originally Hindu and Buddhist female spirits who were often shown singing dancing and scattering petals. In China, Apsaras were known as 'Flying Immortals' (Feitian) and the term came to refer to flying celestials of either gender. In murals from the early Northern Liang and Northern Wei periods, the Apsaras can appear quite un-Chinese, with naked upper bodies, flying scarves and Indian style dhotis. However during the Western Wei, Apsaras are reimagined as Chinese type immortals and often appear together with Chinese deities such as the Queen Mother of the West and the Thunder and Wind Gods. The summit of Apsara drawing at Mogao was during the Tang dynasty. Tang era Apsaras like in the High Tang Cave 320 wear fashionable Tang lady headdresses and long skirts with beautiful patterns and show a natural grace of movement as they scatter petals. The Apsaras after the Tang are in general merely copying the Tang style with their expressions and movements monotonic.

Tang Peak

The great peak of Mogao Cave art was during the Tang (618-906) dynasty when Dunhuang was a major cosmopolitan city on the Silk Road. Around 70 of the caves were constructed at this time and important innovations were reported in visual style, content and sculpture. Dunhuang scholars divide the period into Early (618-704), High (705-780), Middle (781-847) and Late (848-906) Tang periods.

One great achievement of Sui-Tang murals was advances in perspective as proportions between the figures and the backdrops became more rational. The worm's eye frontal perspective of the mural on the northern wall of Cave 172 is justly celebrated. The Tang era also saw the mature development of large detailed narrative paintings, which were frequently illustrations of the sutras and in particular of the Mahayana Buddhist Pure Land. While the preaching Buddha was still at the centre, the scene was often ringed by grand buildings, reflecting great palaces and monasteries of the royal capital Chang'an.

Tang murals at Mogao often contain fascinating details of ordinary life, such as the depiction of a funeral in Cave 148. The well preserved murals of Cave 23 contain farming scenes and a man departing on a business trip. Tang ceilings also display a new expressivity, and a break from the early monotomy of using lotus as the main theme.

Larger Assembly Hall caves were more popular at this time. The cave ceiling of these caves is usually a truncated pyramid, with the decorated inset at the crown of the ceiling, called a *zaojing*, an imitation of a feature of traditional Chinese wooden architecture.

By the Tang dynasty, the Buddha's flanking disciples (usually identified as Ananda and Kasyapa) have lost their earlier Indian look and as in Cave 45 often appear Chinese in splendid robes. In contrast to earlier giant

statues, Tang statues are generally life sized renderings of real people such as beautiful court ladies, generals and monks. Graceful Bodhisattva statues with longated earlobes and plumpness express a classic aesthetic of Tang female beauty.

In the Middle Tang era (781CE-847CE), as the Tang empire was weakened and the Tibetans (Tubo) captured Dunhuang, the Dunhuang statues lost their some of their vigour and charm. However the iconography of Tantric Buddhism, such as the eleven-headed, thousand armed Avalokitesvara, also started to appear frequently in Mogao wall painting during the Tibetan period. Tantric images remained popular in later eras, especially the Yuan dynasty.

The Tang era also saw the growing influence of the school of Mahayana Buddhism, which teaches that there is not one but an infinite number of Buddhas. This insight is expressed in 'thousand Buddha' decorations such as that of the ceiling slopes of Cave 79. The proliferation of the rows of 10cm-20cm miniature Buddhas augurs the more formulaic decoration of the caves in the post-Tang era.

After the Tang

In the Late Tang and the Five Dynasties (907-979), Dunhuang was a fiefdom of local magnates such as the Zhang and the Cao families. Many of the earlier caves were renovated at this time, and new murals were painted over the older ones. Images of family donors appear throughout the caves, particularly in the antechambers.

The art of Dunhuang is generally seen as becoming more stylized after the Tang The post-Tang decline was partly due to the weakening of links with metropolitan China and partly because the art style became more conservative. There are still glories such as the the roof panel of Cave 9 which contains richly detailed images from the four Transformation Sutras. Meanwhile the ninth century Cave 16 is the largest grotto at Mogao.

Ceilings

Ceilings were often the areas of the caves where artists' imaginations enjoyed the freest reign. A good example is the roof of Cave 16 which depicts a phoenix and four dragons with the phoenix placed in the middle. This design is considered a subversive innovation because the dragon, as the symbol of the emperor, should traditionally be centre stage.

Early cave gables were often painted with Chinese-style imitation rafters decorated with lotus. Birds such as peacocks or parrots were sometimes painted between the rafters, while plants, geometric shapes, flames or animals, are seen on the lintels. The flat ceiling at the back of the cave is generally a floral design with a large lotus at its centre.

The Tang dynasty was when a decorated coffer, or zaojing, a Chinese innovation, became popular for the assembly hall types of caves. Early Tang zaojing are particularly creative, such as the spacious coffer of Cave 209, which is filled with grape and pomegranate designs, and creepers symbolizing a big harvest.

In the Five Dynasties period, when many earlier caves were renovated, the colours of the zaojing are more restrained compared with the gaudiness of earlier periods, with a background of green or blue with reddish brown, and the main objects highlighted in gold.

During the Yuan dynasty (1271-1368) seafaring traders manning bulky cargo ships finally superseded the millennial Silk Road. As Silk Road trade ebbed a thousand years of artistry came to an end in Mogao, almost as quickly as it had first began and the place was all but lost in the singing sands.

Rediscovery

In 1900 a Taoist priest named Wang Yanlu settled at Mogao. Wang became the self-appointed guardian of the caves, awarding himself the title of Abbot. While he embarked on his restoration efforts, Abbot Wang discovered thousands of ancient Buddhist manuscripts stored in what is now called the Library Cave.

Almost a decade later a British-Hungarian archeologist named Aurel Stein, renowned as an explorer whose career uncovered lost treasures of Central Asian civilizations, came upon his greatest discovery: Mogao. After surveying the area with characteristic ardour, Stein promised Abbot Wang he would return the sacred scrolls to their spiritual home in India. Instead, they found their way to the British Museum.

Stein was closely followed by French Sinologist Paul Pelliot, who was able to read and translate many of the documents. He too left with a bounty of documents bound for museums in Paris. A host of other foreigners followed before authorities belatedly stepped in to protect what remained of these wonders of antiquity.

To the Chinese, their actions were tantamount to a cultural heist. But the exploits of these pioneers, particularly Stein, were important for the study of the history of Central Asia and Buddhism and the volumes they published on their discoveries brought Mogao out of desert obscurity and to the attention of the world.

Restoration

An equally remarkable story is the restoration effort that has taken place at Mogao over the last century. Chang Shuhong was the first to champion the Mogao cause. He returned from a decade in France and moved his family to Dunhuang in 1943. Work began in 1944 to conserve, record, repair and research the Mogao Grottos. Since then a steady wave of young people have come from all corners of China to contribute their expertise to the programme. Notable figures include DuanWenjie, an art student in Chongqing who after seeing copies of the murals painted by Zhang Daqian, was roused to go to work in Dunhuang. In 1982 Duan became the director of the Cultural Relics Research Institute and in 1984 he became the first director of the Dunhuang Academy. Other remarkable figures include Ouyang Lin who came to Dunhuang accompanied by her lover Shi Wexing. The pair stayed for sixty years painting the murals. Ouyang was still painting Mogao Caves at over 90 years of age!

The restoration work can be divided into two periods. 1950 to 1980 was deemed a period of urgent conservation whilst 1980 to the present has been deemed a period of scientific conservation. Work is on going to document and protect these fragile treasures, which are incredibly vulnerable to the elements. In some of the caves you may notice places where a strip of plaster has been removed from the bottom of a wall mural and replaced by bamboo which ensures a flow of air.

Donors

The history of the Mogao caves is bound up with the history of powerful donor families such as Zhang of Nanyang, Suo of Julu and Cao of Haozhou that formed a political oligarchy and exercised power over religion too as overlords of the monasteries. From the late Tang dynasty it became popular for donors to have their images in the caves. Portraits of donors increased in number and size during the Five Dynasties and the Song.

The Zhangs.
The Zhang family rose to influence in 848 when Zhang Yichao led a rebellion to drive the Tibetans out of Duhuang and restore the region to Tang control. The Zhang family were devout believers in Buddhism and the family instigated a large-scale construction of caves. Images of Zhang Yichao appear in several caves, including Cave 85. Depictions of Zhang and his wife's triumphal procession can be seen in Cave 156.

Monks.
The Zhang family gave special patronage to powerful monks such as Hongbian, who himself sponsored temples such as Cave 365, which was built in 834. After Hongbian died, another monk Zhai Farong built the large cave 85. The cave was completed in five years.

The Caos.
After the Zhang family patriarch Zhang Chengfeng died in 919-920, power in Dunhuang was transferred to the Cao family, who controlled the Hexi area for 122 years. The Caos consolidated their position through alliances with the Uyghurs and the Khotan, which are recorded in murals such as the 2.92m tall portrait of the Khotanese king in Cave 98. After family patriarch CaoYijin died in 950, his son Cao Yuanzhong patronized the construction of the large Cave 61 which contains a giant statue of Manjusri. Images of the elaborately made-up Cao female members also appear in caves built or renovated at this time, such as Caves 61, 98, 100 and 108.

Caves

The ongoing restoration effort means that some caves are closed to the public. Moreover the caves rotate opening times to reduce exposure to humidity and as a result, it is not possible to know in advance which caves will be included on any tour. This section includes a profile of the 50 or so caves at Mogao that as of August 2014 were theoretically open to the public and might be included in a tour. Flash photography is of course banned.

Northern and Southern Dynasties (420CE-580CE)

Cave 246
This Northern Wei Cave was renovated during the Western Xia period. Above the west wall entrance is a preaching scene. The centre of the arched ceiling of the main chamber (like the ceiling of the corridor) comprises entirely of floral designs, while the north and south slopes feature decorative hangings. The lower portions of the west and east walls are patterned with rows of 1000 buddha images interspersed with a few handwritten inscriptions.

Cave 249
This cave's zaojing ceiling is a Western Wei innovation that replaced the earlier central pillar style. This design allow greater freedom for the arrangement of the motifs, which are an eclectic blend of Buddhist images accompanied by gods from both Hindu and Chinese mythology. Look out for the animal headed gods of Wind, Rain, Thunder and Lightning on the west ceiling slope, while the north slope has an image of a winged horse, another symbol of Dunhuang. Around the bottom of the four slopes are landscape and hunting scenes.

Cave 251
This deep cave from the Northern Wei dynasty is dominated by images of the Buddha teaching. The cave has no antechamber and the skylight above the door is positioned so that light floods in and covers the upper body of an East facing Buddha renovated during the Qing. The upper portions of the walls are decorated with images of heavenly musicians while yakshas lurk lower down.

Caves 257

This medium sized cave, which suffered fire damage when White Russian soldiers were imprisoned here in the 1920s, is notable for its pioneering use of narrative painting. The back wall of the cave has a masterful rendering of the well known Buddhist story of Deer King Ruru The parable proceeds from two sides to the centre, where the climax of the story is depicted. The upper portions of the north, south and west walls sing with depictions of heavenly musicians.

Cave 259

This boxy little Northern Wei dynasty grotto (partly renovated during the Song era) is notable for its Chinese style roof with imitation rafters. However there is a strong flavour of India to the statuary, particularly the Boddhisatvas flanking the Buddha as well as the Apsaras in the roof of the niche. The northern wall niches of the main chamber host statues of the Buddha in meditation, evoking the popularity of this pastime in northern China during this period.

Cave 296

The small but exquisite cave is of Northern Zhou provenance, although murals such as the depiction of the Medicine Buddha on the ceiling of the antechamber ar Five Dynasties overlays. The niche statues date from the Qing dynasty. The most notable feature of the main chamber are the narrative paintings on the slopes of the caisson roof which offer moral guidance for Silk Road traders: the catechisms include planting trees, building bridges and caring for a sick camel.

Cave 428

Dating back to the early 6th century, this is the largest cave constructed during the Northern Zhou dynasty but was restored during the Five Dynasties period by the Cao family, whose donor images graffiti the corridor. The main chamber layout has a central stupa housing statues of a preaching Buddha in the lotus position and two disciples. Topping the cave is a distinctive Chinese style gabled roof whose panels are embellished with images of monkey, plants, deer, birds and peacocks.

Sui Dynasty (581CE-618CE)

Cave 244
Redecoration took place during the Western Xia, evident in the floral designs around the entrance and in the corridor, as well as the miniature Buddhas around the door. There are also donor paintings from the Five Dynasties in this cave. The main hall's ceiling still bares wooden structural remains left by the Sui. On the west, south and north walls are statues of the Buddha in different guises, flanked by two Bodhisattvas. The east wall mural depicts nine flying figures, celestial mansions and five cross-legged sitting Buddhas.

Cave 292
The anteroom and corridor suggest several successive dynasties redecorated and embellished the cave. Much of the main hall is festooned with the thousand Buddha motif. The niche on the east-facing side of the central column contains a standing Buddha statue. The niches on the north, south and west faces of the column shelter statues of a meditating Buddha and two disciples. The north, south and west walls, as well as the east wall around the door, feature the same mural, depicting flying musicians and celestial palaces.

Cave 390
Some of the statues of this cave are not original; they were restored during the Qing dynasty. However the roof is exceptionally well preserved with obvious Sui characteristic including the deep red colour background. The Thousand Buddha motif coats the ceiling, framing a lotus flower in the centre. The Buddha is depicted teaching in the murals with a diverse array of colourful canopies sheltering the congregation. Lower down on the walls there is a donor image from the Five Dynasties period.

Cave 397

Renovation took place during the Five Dynasties period, evident in the anteroom and corridor where we find a mural depicting a history of Buddhism in Khotan. In the main hall the Great Conception, when an elephant touched Shakyamuni's mother, is depicted in double-recessed niche, a style typical of the Sui and Early Tang. An aura has been painted around the Buddha's head, resembling a flaming headdress. On the ceiling the three hares are depicted running in a circle, a symbol of the Christian Trinity. It is believed the design travelled down Silk Road from the West. Geometric Iranian designs are also evident in the frescos.

Cave 407

Abbot Wang who dug holes in the walls to create a passageway damaged the corridor. The three hares insignia on ceiling, believed to be a Christian symbol, is framed by lotus designs and depictions of Arhats. The niche on the west wall shelters statues of a Buddha, a disciple and four Bodhisattvas cast in Sui. There's a statue of a Bodhisattva cast in the Qing as well. The fresco behind the statues depicts angels playing harps, flutes and pipes. The Thousand Buddha motif is widespread in the cave.

Cave 419

One of the grandest cave shrines at Mogao is also a clear example of the national religion being harnessed to exhibit imperial power. In the anteroom, above the entrance of the west wall are depictions of precious offerings, two flying figures, and seven Buddhas that date to the Western Xia Dynasty. In the main hall there's a statue of the cross-legged Buddha, a graceful style that was propagated by the first Sui emperor as a guise to be used throughout the empire. The four attendant statues of disciples and bodhisattvas are child-like by comparison. Flesh tones of the statues have, alas, blackened due to oxidisation of the lead

pigment. There is a marvellous mural depicting a preaching scene, framed by a Thousand Buddha motif.

Cave 420

Three walls of this assembly hall style cave have statue bearing niches. On the west wall we see a new feature, a double recess, which can house more statues. The Buddha with two disciples and four Bodhisattvas are in the main niche, while the Buddha and two Bodhisattvas are in each of the north and south niches on either side of the cave. The truncated pyramid ceiling is adorned with a busy but beautiful fresco depicting several interwoven narratives from the Lotus Sutra.

Cave 427

This largest of the Sui grottos has a traditional wood pillar entrance with evocative sloping tile eaves. Inside there is an antechamber which according to an inscription was built during the Northern Song dynasty. However, the six statues, including four Heavenly Kings and two Dharma Protectors are thought to date back to the time of the Sui dynasty. The main chamber's central pillar is festooned with Thousand Buddhas images while before it are statues depicting the Buddha and two Bodhisattvas. On either wall is a triad of Buddhas most commonly thought to depict the Buddha past, present and future.

Early Tang (618CE-704CE)

Cave 71
The four slopes of the ceiling bear the Thousand Buddhas motif. The niche on the west wall contains statues of a cross-legged sitting Buddha flanked by two Bodhisattvas. The north wall is illustrated with the Maitreya Sutra while the mural on the south wall depicts the Amitabha Sutra, one of the primary sutras upheld in the Pure Land Buddhist schools.

Cave 96
This is one of the most famous caves in Mogao, and for good reason. Also known as the Big Buddha cave, it contains a thirty metre tall seated Maitreya statue. China's great Tang empress Wu Zetian sponsored the cave construction. The statue was cast in the early Tang but repaired during the early twentieth century Republic period. This is evident in the iconic nine-story facade built into the cliff face.

Cave 202
Comprising of an anteroom, corridor and main hall, this cave was first completed in the early Tang period though refurbishments followed right the way up until the Qing dynasty. While the outer sections contain Song dynasty murals, the main hall has work dating to the early and mid Tang, and Song as well as Tibetan influences in the depiction of the Buddha. The niche on the west wall has statues of a cross-legged sitting Buddha, accompanied by two Arhats, Bodhisattvas and Vajra warriors. The south wall illustrates the Paradise of Maitreya. The north wall features the Buddha of the Ten Directions attending a meeting.

Cave 203

The antechamber and corridor contain work added during the Song dynasty and though the main hall dates to the Tang we see a strong Sui influence. In the centre of the ceiling there are lotus designs while the four slopes are covered by decorative hangings and the Thousand Buddha motif. The niche on the west wall has statues of standing Buddha leaning on a mountain and two Bodhisattvas. The north and south walls are painted with preaching scenes with miniature Buddhas and flying figures on either side. Above the entrance on the east wall are four rows of miniature Buddhas, a set of seven Buddhas and offering of vessels painted during the Song Dynasty.

Cave 204

This cave displays several typical Sui characteristics, notably a double-recessed niche. On the west wall there`s a statue of Buddha, two Arhats, and four Bodhisattvas, which have been poorly repaired during the Qing dynasty. Xuanzang`s pilgrimage is depicted in a mural. The famous Tang monk's epic 15-year journey to India and back concluded with a stay in the Mogao grottos, where he deposited many Sanskrit manuscripts.

Cave 323

This medium-sized cave's antechamber, corridor and the entrance wall were all renovated in the Five Dynasties and the Western Xia. A new layer of mural was painted on parts of the walls during the renovations, although originals on the north and south walls, the ceilings and niche, survive. Tang landscape painting reached its zenith around this time and this is apparent in the main chamber. Rivers depicted in the murals are applied to great effect in joining and distinguishing different scenes in the story of Buddhism in China, including the exploits of Han explorer Zhang Qian on the northern wall.

Cave 328

The highlight of Cave 328 is five incredibly lifelike, seventh-century statues. The central icon is considered a masterwork in depicting all the principle attributes of the Buddha. Next are disciple Sakyamuni's younger cousin Amanda and Mahakasypa. The two Bodhisattvas are without fixed genders, mixing and matching sexual characteristics. The original painting inside the niche is seventh century but there`s an eleventh century repainting outside the niche. A Song dynasty stupa was moved into the grotto from outside in order to protect it. On the roof we see a protective tantric symbol.

Cave 329

Boasting one of the most lavish ceilings in Mogao, the grotto's Thousand Buddha motif, signifying the omnipresence of the Buddha, winds around a centrepiece of lotus flowers and celestial beings. The south wall illustrates the Amitabha Sutra below which twenty-three female donors have been painted during the Five Dynasties. The north wall`s mural illustration of the Maitreya Sutra exhibits damage inflicted by American explorer Landon Warner.

Cave 331

This cave was renovated during the Five Dynasties and again during the Qing dynasty. The niche on the west wall shelters statues of a cross-legged sitting Buddha, two disciples and two bodhisattvas. The south wall illustrates the Maitreya Sutra, beneath which there are nineteen female donors and twenty-seven female attendants. The north wall illustrates the Amitabha Sutra, below which are depictions of the male donors. The murals on the north and south sides of the entrance depict preaching scenes.

Cave 332

This cave was decorated soon after the Sui dynasty. There's a big square pillar in the main hall. Three sets of statues are presented in the configuration of present, past and future Buddhas. Right at the back of the hall is a seven metre long "sleeping" Buddha, repainted during the Qing dynasty. The narrative story of the last teaching is depicted in an exquisite mural on the adjacent wall. Here we see the Buddha reaching Nirvana, the funeral parade and cremation, and after the cremation a near war fought over the relics of his body.

Cave 334

Poor Qing dynasty restoration has given the statues in this cave strange, cartoonish appearances. The painting behind the statues is an original, dating back to the seventh century. The colours are well preserved with potent greens and blues. Sakyamuni is depicted in teaching posture, the painting depicts the Transformation Sutra, an unusual and complex painting to position in the niche. Around the sixth or seventh century esoteric Buddhism arrived in Dunhuang and we see esoteric, or tantric Buddhist elements in the murals, signifying protection. The ceiling exhibits a beautiful lotus design.

Cave 335

Though this cave dates back to the Early Tang it was renovated during Middle Tang, Song, Yuan and Qing dynasties. In the main hall the ceiling centres around peony flowers while the four slopes are covered by floral motifs, decorative hangings and the thousand Buddha motif. The niche on the west wall shelters statues of a cross-legged sitting Buddha and a disciple, both of which were cast during the Tang dynasty. The other five statues of a disciple and four bodhisattvas are of Qing dynasty vintage. The north side has a preaching scene drawn during Middle Tang and below it are the figures of four Bodhisattvas painted in Yuan dynasty times.

Cave 340

The centre of the ceiling shows floral designs. The Thousand Buddha motif and decorative hangings cover the four slopes. The niche on the west wall contains statues of Buddha, two disciples and two Bodhisattvas cast in Early Tang. The statues of two Bodhisattvas date back to the Qing. Above the entrance of the east wall six Bodhisattvas accompany a portrait of eleven-headed Avalokitesvara, said to exhibit the compassion of all Buddhas. We see block painting on the rear wall, a Greco style that travelled down the Silk Road.

High Tang (705-781)

Cave 23
Although heavily renovated during the Middle Tang and the Five Dynasties, this cave holds a number of well-preserved original murals that offer precious glimpses of ordinary life in Tang times. The northern wall features farming scenes of both sunshine and rain. The southern wall relates the saga of a man bidding farewell to his wife and leaving on a business trip. The man is shown setting off along the Silk Road, where his group of traders are first attacked by bandits and then rescued by Guanyin. On the roof slopes are images of the seven treasures of Buddhism: elephant, horse, general, Queen, Minister, jewel, and wheel of truth.

Cave 45

This High Tang cave, normally off-limits, is considered a highlight of Mogao. The classic Tang caisson ceiling in the main chamber has a centre of floral designs while the slopes are covered with miniature Buddhas. Among the cave's many treasures is a rare early depiction of the death penalty. The narrative painting shows the convict is about to be decapitated, but at the last minute he confesses and his life is spared. The south wall mural depicts the 33 manifestations of Guanyin from the Lotus Sutra, while to the south of the main entrance is a portrait of Thousand Armed Avalokitesvara drawn in the High Tang. The rich colourful clothes of the statues show the good life of monks in the Tang and the attention to detail is also impressive; for example the finger joints are enlarged from carrying heavy weights, reflecting a time when it was popular for 'bold types' to carry heavy weapons.

Cave 46

The chess board and floral patterns on the ante-chamber ceiling were laid down in the Five Dynasties, while the Buddha in the centre of the corridor ceiling is of Song origin. The life sized main chamber statues with their elongated earlobes and plumpness pulse with a classic High Tang style and embody the Tang perspective that God is just like us. The niche in the north wall of the contains an array of standing Medicine Buddhas.

Cave 79

Entry to this High Tang cave, renovated during the Five Dynasties period, is through a flight of steps leading to a basement. The badly worn walls of the antechamber contain rare tantric images, while fragments of donor images are preserved in the corridor. The main chamber statues exhibit characteristic Tang plumpness and facial individuality, although they were brightly repainted in the Qing dynasty. Once red Thousand Buddha images on the ceiling slopes are now brown as a result of oxidization. The ceiling is decorated by familiar lotus and three dimensional floral designs but there are intricate details in the corners, including little babies making offerings to Buddha.

Cave 103

The antechamber harbours two well decorated mini grottos (104, 105.) The main chamber is best known for its eighth century landscape paintings in the 'blue-green' style which was celebrated in the High Tang Court before the technique was lost to history. Although no examples are preserved outside of the Mogao murals. Sakyamuni on the south wall embodies the benefits of worshipping the Dharma. On the eastern wall is a vey Chinese looking Vimalakirti, while below him are portraits of princes of different nationalities. The graffiti left by Russian soldiers that were detained here in the 1920s offers evidence of other visitors from afar.

Cave 148

This coffin shape of this second floor cave dating from the High Tang implies the finality of physical death. The shape of the cave, the main painting and the central icon are all related to Nirvana. The cave was built in the eleventh year of the Dali Era (777) of the Tang dynasty and two accounts of the building and renovation of the cave by Li Dabin and his descendants are inscribed in the ante-room. Above the entrance on the East wall is a Tantric influenced portrait of the thousand armed, thousand eyed Avalokitesvara (Guanyin.) The Western wall contains a rare depiction of a Chinese funeral and one favourite detail is a rooster on the coffin.

Cave 171

This small High Tang cave was renovated during the Song and Qing dynasties. The main chamber north and south walls depict karma teachings of the Amitayurbavana Sutra. The detail of these stories exemplifies the realistic style of Tang story telling, although the original pink and red shades are browned off thanks to oxidization. The West wall niche contains statues of a cross-legged sitting Buddha and two Bodhisattvas cast in the Tang. However the statues of the four disciples are of Qing vintage. The centre of the caisson ceiling abounds with clusters of High Tang flowers.

Cave 172

This High Tang cave is noted for its northern wall mural of the Western Pure Land. The frontal perspective is very influential, offering what appears to be a worm's eye view. Apsaras flying around the stupa are clearly influenced by the Western (ie Indian) style, and the feminine Boddhisatvas with their narrow waists also look very Indian. On the southern wall a portrait of the monastery draws us in and in contrast to the usual detachment, the Amitaddha Buddha appears focused on the audience. The pipa playing girl on the southern wall is another symbol of Dunhuang.

Tibetan (781CE-847CE)

Cave 231

In the corridor the ceiling has been painted with a thousand-armed and thousand-eyed Avalokitesvara while the walls have portraits of the Cao clan added during the Song dynasty. In the main hall the ceiling shows a lion and round petal lotus designs in the centre. The niche on the west wall contains statues of a cross-legged sitting Buddha and two disciples, one of which was carved in the Qing.

Cave 237

The antechamber and corridor were largely redecorated during the Western Xia, evident in the ceiling mural, which shows coiled dragons, chessboard and floral designs. The south wall of the corridor features male donors and attendants while the north wall features two female donors drawn in the Western Xia era, all of which are faded or damaged. On the ceiling of the main hall you can see a three hares symbol, alleged to have been adopted from Christianity. The niche contains five statues and a horse-hoof shaped Buddha throne cast during the Qing dynasty. Several prominent sutras are depicted in the wall murals.

Late Tang (848CE – 907CE)

Cave 9
The roof slopes of this exceptionally well preserved cave contain richly detailed images from the Maitreya Sutra and the Avatamsaka Sutra. The Maitreya Sutra scene shows ladies in the Maitreya Pure Land getting married at 500 years old. The painting is noted for its depictions of many non-Han people, including Koreans and Tibetans. On the northern wall there is a rendering of the transformations of the Magic Competition, a popular theme of the Tang Mogao murals. The donor of this cave, a member of the Li family, was the son in law of the hero Zhang Yichao, who drove the Tibetans out of Dunhuang. However tensions and power struggles soon arose between the two families.

Cave 11
This Qing dynasty grotto may be found on the other side of the antechamber from Cave 13. The north wall features a set of three statues and a painting of a screen with clouds and dragons.

Cave 12
The statue group of this medium sized Late Tang Cave is of Qing dynasty provenance. The southern wall of the main chamber has a well preserved Lotus Sutra. Look out for a lion and a lotus in the centre of the inverted pyramid roof ringed by slopes decorated with Thousand Buddha images. Images of the Suo family donors can be found above the door and at the base of the niche.

Cave 13
This mini grotto in the antechamber of Cave 12 is Late Tang but the statue in the niche on the south wall was carved during the Qing. The caisson ceiling features camellia flowers in the centre.

Cave 16

This ninth century is the largest grotto at Mogao but at 16m deep it also suffers from damp. The Hongbian Monk, aligned to the powerul Zhang family, was the donor of this cave. The wall murals are eleventh century restorations. The roof inset shows a phoenix and four dragons, with the phoenix is placed in the centre, a revolutionary design, because in Chinese culture the dragon is the symbol of the emperor, while the phoenix represents the empress. However the phoenix as a guardian of the Buddha can eat the dragon. The cave is one of those to have benefited from a pioneering conservation technique that involves replacing the 16cm thick bottom layer of plaster with moisture absorbing bamboo which allows air to circulate. The eyes of some of the statues in this cave were scratched out by Muslim iconoclasts.

Cave 17. The Library Cave

The reasons why about 45,000 documents came to be sealed in this 10m square north facing alcove remain obscure. The cave itself was cut in the 5th year of the Xuanzong era of the Tang Dynasty (52CE) as a memorial cave of Monk Hongbian. Full of manuscripts when it was discovered by Taoist priest Wang Yuanlu in June 1900, the cave is empty again now. The manuscripts found in the cave date from the fourth to the early eleventh centuries and are a treasure trove of works ranging from history and maths to folk songs and dance. It is speculated that monks sealed the documents in this cave before the anticipated capture of Dunhuang by Tangut incursors. The monks fled to avoid the war and later the secret of the library cave was forgotten. From 1907 onwards, Wang began to sell the manuscripts to Western explorers, particularly Aurel Stein and Paul Pelliot. They are now scattered in institutions across the world, including the British Museum and Bibliothèque Nationale de France as well as the National Library of China. The manuscripts are being digitalized by the Dunhuang International Project and they represent a resource of inestimable value for learning about ancient eastern cultures. Many languages are represented including Sanskrit, Sogdian and Old Uyghur, although most of the manuscripts are in the Chinese and Tibetan languages.

Western Xia
(1038CE – 1279CE)

Cave 25

Sixteen flying musicians swirl around the caisson ceiling. The west, north and south slopes display illustrations of the Avatamsaka Sutra, also known in English as the Flower Sutra. A floral motif on the ceiling resonates with this moniker. Five statues and two celestial animals in the west wall niche were sculpted in the Qing dynasty.

Cave 55

The impressive stone dais of this huge cave built under the stewardship of the local Cao clan boasts three Maitreya Buddhas, three Bodhisattvas, an old Arhat and two Devarajas (a fourth Bodhisattva and Ananda are missing). During the Late Tang dynasty many more sutras had found their way into the popular vernacular and this is reflected in the staggering 16 distinct sutras which are vividly illustrated on the walls of the cave. Some of the sutras depicted, like the Linkavatara Sutra, are very rare and are among the great treasures of Mogao.

Sanwei Mountain

(三危山, Sānwēi Shān)

Opposite Mogao is the ominously named "Three Dangers" Mountain, so deemed because its three peaks appeared precarious to the ancient Chinese. The early settlement of Dunhuang was originally named Sanwei after the mountain. In 366AD the monk Le Zun supposedly founded the Mogao caves after having a vision of a thousand Buddhas at Sanwei. Sanwei Mountain became an important holy site hereafter, adorned with stupas and temples.

Much of Sanwei's religious heritage has been lost to history, or reconstructed by the Dunhuang Sun Tourist Group, distinctly devoid of the fabled artistry of the Tang. But the Sanwei Mountain Scenic Area is still very much worth a visit, especially if you want to stretch your legs and enjoy some scenery after a tour of ancient caves.

Visiting

The state of the road through the scenic area prohibits saloon cars. Only 4X4s can negotiate the uneven lay of the land. But the spectacular landscape is best enjoyed on foot. This hard, craggy, brown desert is a far cry from the drifting Dunes of Mingsha. The stony land even sustains some life as Chinese Aspens line the route, and occasionally, pheasants can be seen pottering about in groups.

The first manmade object you pass is a set of statues depicting a scene from classical novel *Journey to the West*. Further into the Scenic Area there's a spattering of made-to-look old dynastic gates, temples and stupas, as well as an ancient well from which you can still drink.

The scenic area's climax is a giant Buddha statute set against a glorious mountain backdrop opposite the Nanshan Temple. This is the principle site of worship. The temple has three resident caretakers, who offer water and sustenance to thirsty pilgrims. The courtyard shimmers with the flapping prayers flags beneath which vegetables are grown in a private garden.

2 Crescent Moon Lake (月牙泉, Yùeyá Quán) and Mingshan Hill (鸣沙山, Míngshā Shān)

Located just 6km south of Dunhuang city, and visible from downtown, Mingsha is less a hill and more a sea of mighty sand dunes. This is desert landscape of the imagination: golden sand dunes cascading towards the horizon. Except remarkably, the area is not entirely parched. A small oasis bubbles to the surface amongst the dunes.

The Spring has long been remarked on by travellers and the earliest written record is in an Eastern Han (BCE25-BCE220) book, *Xin's Annals of the Qin Lands*. "Hexi has a sand hill, the peak high and perilous, beyond stone mountains, the sand coarse and yellow, the hill unchanging. To the south of the hill is a spring, a well in the desert, whose water has flowed through the ages, the sand cannot fill it."

History and Legend

Though many over the centuries have likened the lake to the eye or mouth of a beautiful woman, the most enduring myth is that the lake is a perfect half-moon which has fallen from heaven to Earth. During the Qing dynasty the name Yueyaquan or Moon Crescent Spring was adopted.

Beside the lake is the giant dune called Mingsha, which means literally "Chiming Sands" in reference to a curious natural phenomenon. The singing sands of the Gobi Desert were said to haunt Silk Road traders, conjuring ghoulish myths of a tormented desert. What they were actually hearing was the wind whipping the sand from the dunes, which creates a soft, distant hum.

Geology

Moon Crescent Spring is estimated to be two thousand years old but due to its location in a depression, prevailing winds carry sand away from it, largely sparing it the ravages of desertification. That said, the Moon Crescent Spring is not entirely the natural phenomena it pertains to be. Over the later half of the twentieth century, water levels measurably dropped, promoting the local government to intervene in 2006 to restore them. Today the Crescent Spring swells with cobalt water again and is flanked by a majestic Crescent Lake Temple, which acts as a rest area offering food, refreshment and shade.

Getting There and Staying at the Dunes

Mingsha Hill is easy to reach from the city proper via taxi or bus and is included on many tour operator itineraries. It is close enough to the city centre that many decide to cycle to the mighty dunes. Alternatively you can reside right next-door to Mingsha. The main thoroughfare Mingshan Road has several notable luxury hotels including the Friendship Hotel. Just off Shazhou South Road there's a cluster of hostels with Charley Johng's Dune Guesthouse being the most well known amongst the backpacker crowd. Many of the smaller establishments offer traditional northern Chinese kang rooms while others provide wood cabin accommodation. Though you might have to walk to frequent certain amenities, staying in a cabin is a perfect way to enjoy the spectacle of the desert at night, the star-filled universe visible in the unpolluted sky overhead while you sip a refreshing Yellow River Beer.

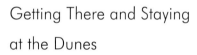

Visiting

The Mingsha Hill Scenic Area has become something of a tourist snare in recent years offering a host of activities designed to give tour groups a taste of the desert. In China, this means crowds! Therefore, choose your time carefully. Weekends and national holidays are best avoided, and midday can be searingly hot in the desert. In fact, the best way to enjoy the stunning spectacle of the Moon Crescent Spring is at sunrise or sunset when the luminosity of the spring and the surrounding sand dunes conjures a mystic ambience that recalls the many odes dedicated to the spring. This is a great way to beat the crowds and see Mingsha Hill and the Crescent Lake at their best.

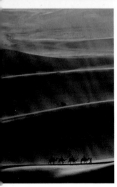

Camping and Camel Hikes

Many hotels around Mingsha offer camping trips into the desert (though not in the allotted scenic area itself.) Camel Hikes are priced at around RMB400 / day including a guide and tent. There's a longer camel route from Mingsha to Mogao Caves but it is not particularly recommended as the distance is considerable. One can also camp and picnic in the desert.

Folk Culture Museum

The Mingsha Hill Folk Culture Museum, situated by the entrance to the Minsha area, exhibits textiles, home furnishings and indigenous handicrafts. There's also a small theatre-come-restaurant with daily folk-themed performances. *Admission: free.*

Outdoor Activities

A number of activities are offered for those who would like to experience the dunes in a more interactive way. Most of the services are being touted at the entrance to the dunes by the carpark.

View From on High: The Mingsha Hill Scenic Area boasts its own mini-airstrip. That's right, for those willing to pay for a thrilling ride, not to mention a spectacular arial view of the desert, there are microlight aeroplanes and even helicopter rides on offer. *Helicopter: From RMB280/person; Microlight: From RMB1760/person.*

Desert Racer: The cascading sand dunes are not easy to negotiate on foot. However, on quad bikes or in jeeps the sandy waves offer fantastic high speed fun. *From RMB300/person.*

Camel Trekking: The camel's days of shifting freight from Cathay to Rome might have passed but evolution has made these resilient beasts ideally suited to desert life. The two humped Bactrian Camel native to do Dunhuang can go months without water, enduring extreme temperatures. Most importantly their padded feet enable them to walk on sand dunes with ease. Riders follow a set trail through the scenic area but the lurching motion of the creatures and the sheer number of people taking a ride will conjure the illusion that you are part of a genuine camel train. The route first takes you to the top of the dunes where you can ascend a final steep slope on foot to admire the view and enjoy an optional sand slide. You then remount your camel which will take you down and around to the Moon Crescent Lake. *RMB100/person.*

Slip-sliding Away: Sand sliding is another popular desert activity. There's a choice of two possible means to race down the dunes. The first is a on a rather leisurely bamboo sledge. The second, preferred by thrill seekers, is to hire a rubber tube for a far more rapid dune decent. *RMB15/bamboo, RMB25/rubber.*

3 Western Thousand Buddha Caves · Yumenguan · Han Great Wall · Yadan

This route, heading southwest through the desert to Yumenguan, covers some of the greatest highlights that Dunhuang has to offer, from the secret treasures of the Western Thousand Buddha Caves, to the poetic desiccation of Yumenguan and the Han Great Wall, and the eerie desert wilderness of Yadan. Restaurants and shops are few indeed on this road so it is suggested to bring whatever victuals you will need.

Western Thousand Buddha Caves

(西千佛洞 , Xī Qiānfó Dòng)

On the north bank of the Dang River 35km from Dunhuang City is a Buddhist cave temple site known as the Western Thousand Buddha Caves. While many caves have been ravaged by floods and collapse, about 16 are extant, although only four or five of these are currently open to the public. The caves, a 40 minute drive from downtown Dunhuang, still make a good place to break a journey to Yumenguan. The caves are located within striking distance of the Yangguan Pass and were a popular stopping off point for traders and monks on the southern route of the Silk Road.

History

While the Mogao Caves hosted communities of monks, the Western Thousand Buddha Caves had more of a practical function. Itinerants departing for the world beyond China's borders, or returning from a long tour of the Western Regions, would stop here to relax and pay devotion.

According to a Five Dynasties manuscript found in the Mogao Library Cave, the origin of the Western Thousand Buddha Caves dates back to the Han dynasty. This makes them older than the Mogao Caves themselves.

Visiting the Caves

A handy landmark near the turnoff to the caves is the Sleeping Buddha Hill, named for its nirvanic shape. From the carpark a staircase descends a cliff to a wooded river valley which is refreshingly cool on a hot day. The caves are arrayed along the cliff to the left of the staircase while the small ticket kiosk waits at the bottom of the steps by the entrance to the wood. No English speaking guides are available. However the wooded valley is a pleasant place to rest or picnic. It is also worth walking a few minutes through the small wood to the Dang River, which is majestic as it swaggers through a stony plain with cliffs rising behind. *Foreigners pay 40 yuan for a twenty minute tour of five caves. Tickets are RMB30 for Chinese nationals and RMB15 for students and seniors.*

The Caves

16 decorated caves house around 800 sqm of wall murals and 34 statues dating from the Northern Wei to the late Yuan and early Ming dynasties. The general quality is beneath that found at Mogao but there are several treasures. The caves are grouped into three sections. The handful of caves currently open to the public are all in the main group, Caves 1-16, at the western end of the cliff.

Cave 3 (Early Tang)
Thoroughly renovated in the Western Xia dynasty, little of this cave's original Tang decoration remains. The main niche Buddha is a Preaching Buddha of Ming provenance and the east wall niche hosts a similar figure. A tiger lurks in one western wall niche. The ceiling slopes are decorated with a familiar floral pattern. The antechamber is a Sui dynasty refit.

Cave 4 (Sui)
On the east side of the antechamber is a small grotto which can't be entered. The murals are Ming and the large and robust statues with slender eyebrows are Qing. The main chamber was restored in the Tang and Republic of China periods. One curiosity is the cave number inscription made in the early twentieth century by a famous artist and calligraphist Zhang Daqian.

Cave 5 (Northern Wei)
This Northern Wei cave has retained its original decorations. The walls are covered with Thousand Buddha images although the roof is naked. The Asparas on the east side of the stupa are of Indian and masculine appearance. A happy looking Maitreya holds court at the front. Dancers cavort around the top of the walls, while Yakshas and Yakshis in red and black lurk lower down at the bottom

of the north wall. One of the most famous features of this cave is an inscription written by a Buddhist disciple called Tanang for his dead grandparents and parents.

Cave 6 (Northern Zhou)

On the lowest part of the east wall and the square stupa are images of this cave's sponsors: silk road traders prudently investing in their spiritual futures. A Preaching Buddha dominates the east side of the stupa while Asparas flutter at the top. Despite the sponsors' generosity, cheap materials were evidently used in the painting of the roof, resulting in colour instability. The western wall displays a mural of the Buddha's enlightenment.

Cave 7 (Northern and Southern Dynasties)

The late Tang or Five Dynasties back wall mural features a reclining Buddha surrounded by disciples. The disciples' different facial expressions reflect their attitudes towards nirvana. The floral patterned cave ceiling was created during the Western Wei era but the niche statues are Qing. The cave is noted for its vivid depictions of Asparas, while the walls are decorated by miniature buddhas. On the panel to the right of the door is a well drawn Tang dynasty mural of a Preaching Buddha with two Boddhisatvas. At the bottom are sponsor images.

Yumenguan – The Jade Gate Pass (玉门关 , Yùménguān)

About 105km from downtown Dunhuang, Yumenguan was established between the 2nd century BCE and 3rd century CE as one of two important Han Dynasty border gates overseeing long-distance traffic along the northern Silk Road. Situated on the south bank of Shule River, the Jade Gate Pass with its access to a vital watersupply, was an obvious place to establish a strategic border checkpoint. All caravans travelling through Dunhuang were required to pass through either Yumenguan or the other Han dynasty pass of Yangguan, 68km away.

Today Yumenguan consists of three main sites: the Small Fangpan Castle (the border office), where those crossing the border got their travel documents stamped, the Big Fangpan Castle (Storehouse) where grain was kept for the soldiers on border duty, and stretches of the Han era Great Wall.

History

The Gobi Desert and Mongolian Steppe created a natural boundary to the Chinese Empire that wouldn't be surmounted until relatively recently. The "Western Regions" as the ancient Chinese dubbed the lands beyond China were as much enshrouded in myth as they were coated in rock and sand. It was from this infertile, lawless expanse that the Xiongnu would hone into view – horse riding nomads that were the first of many "barbarian" peoples to raid the Middle Kingdom over the centuries. By the time of the Han dynasty the concept of Tian Xia "All Under Heaven" was rooted in the psyche of the nation. The Emperor, also known as the son of heaven, ruled the civilised world. Beyond lay a realm of mystery and danger.

Yet it was through the burgeoning silk trade with distant Empires that the court in Chang'an (present day Xi'an) was swelling the imperial coffers. Dependent on foreign trade, the Han sent expeditions into Central Asia, the most notable of which being Zhang Qian's imperial envoy, beginning in the 2nd century BC. Zhang's legendary odyssey, documented in Siam Qian's *Records of the Great Historian*, helped open-up much of what would become known as the Silk Road.

In order to extend the dominion of heaven right to edge of China's most important trade routes, the Han expanded the Great Wall to the tip of the Jinxi Corridor, reaching a location just 105km to the west of Dunhuang, a place known as Yunmenguan, the Jade Gate Pass.

The pass became the gateway to the northern Silk Road route across the Gobi desert. Originally called 'the castle,' the pass was later called the Jade Gate Pass because of the number of jade caravans that passed through it. The name attained a romantic resonance for generations of Chinese and occurs in many poems by past masters. After the Silk Road fell into disrepair the location of the pass was forgotten for a millenium until it was rediscovered in the early twentieth century.

Border Office
(小方盘城, XiǎofāngPánchéng)

The best preserved building on the Pass is the Small Fangpan Castle. This military command centre is a remarkable example of the reach and sophistication of Han bureaucracy. The ruin still boasts four walls almost ten metres in height. Small Fangpan Castle is 26.4 metres long, when measured from north to south, while its east to west walls are 24 metres in length. An entrance gate allows visitors to explore the interior space, where the border office would have overseen international trade 2,000 years ago. Visitors can gaze out across the landscape through the remnants of a distinctive north-facing window.

In front of Small Fangpan Castle there are the dusty remains of an affiliated house. Overlooking the Yangshuihaizi Salt Lake, the foundations offer the must-have Yumenguan photo, with the beguilingly desert landscape as a backdrop.

There is also an affiliated museum with some bilingual, Chinese-English plaques telling the epic history of Yumenguan, including the adventures of Zhang Qian, the first official diplomat of the Han court to bring back reliable information of the nations and people of the "Western Regions". As well as informative plaques, the museum houses a collection of ancient articles found at the Yumen Pass site including sackcloth, a wooden fine tooth comb and a leather belt.

The museum also tells of Yumenguan's associations with a list of poets who wrote odes to the Pass. These include such literary greats as Wang Changling, Hu Zeng, Zhang Yanghang and Li Bai. The poetic reverence for Yumen Pass illustrates the place the Jade Gate occupies in the popular imagination of the Chinese as a doorway to the unknown world beyond the Celestial Kingdom.

By Wang Changling (698-756)

Qinghai clouds shroud the snowy peaks,
A remote town faces the Yumen Gate.
After endless battles our golden armour is worn.
With Loulan unbeaten we'll never return.

87

Storehouse
(大方盘城 , Dàfāng Pánchéng)

Located 11km to the northwest of the Small
Fangpan Castle, the Big Fangpan Castle is in
essence the ruins of a Han Dynasty warehouse
where food and supplies would have been
stored for the men stationed at Jade Gate Pass.
Also known as the Great Wall Granary, the site
is 134.8 meters long from east to west and 18
meters wide from north to south. It is located
on parched tableland, affording visitors a
fantastic panorama of the wilderness beyond.

Han Great Wall
(汉长城 , Hàn Chángchéng)

The remnants of the Han Great Wall stretch across the landscape near the Jade Gate Pass. It is particularly well preserved near the Big Fangpan Castle, though dispel images of the mighty stone dragon-spine that tops the mountains north of Beijing. That part of the Great Wall was built much later, under the stewardship of the Ming dynasty. Outside Dunhuang the original Great Wall has been largely reduced to a yellowish brown furrow in the desert. But it is still easy to distinguish from the natural contours in the landscape.

Along this ancient battlement, where Han troops were deployed to ward of marauding nomads, one can still make-out many of the 20 beacons that line the Wall. 17 are set from east to west, three from north to south with the Danggu Beacon Tower next to the Yangshuihaizi Lake one of the best examples. The beacon was made from earth and reeds and still stands at an impressive 7.2 metres. Sticky rice was added to the Han wall's mortar compound, helping to account for its durability. Nearby, one can see piles of reeds that would have been used as building materials or to transmit signals during wartime.

Yadan National Geopark
(敦煌雅丹国家地质公园, Yǎdān Guójiā Dìzhí Gōnguán)

While the name of the Gobi Desert might conjure up images of a stoney wilderness, the desert around Dunhuang is a dynamic, diversely beautiful place. Located 180 kilometres from town, the Yadan National Geopark is probably the best place to enjoy the eerie majesty of the surrounding area's unique geology.

Covering 398km², the Yadan National Geopark is the largest of its kind in China. Following tradition, locals have likened the shapes of rocks to certain animals, bestowing names line Stone Bird and The Golden Lion Welcoming His Guests to notable outcroppings. However the eerie effect is heightened by the unusual black sand between the rocks. Deep in the park is an area known as Ghost Town which, as its name suggests, is the most haunting, the silence only permeated by the soul-stirring whistle of the Singing Sands.

Geology and History

The Yadan region was first documented by Swedish explorer Sven Hedin. Between 1893 and 1935 Hedin led four notable expeditions to Central Asia. The fourth, which began in 1927, was a Sino-Swedish survey aimed at investigating the meteorological, topological and human history of the Gobi Desert. Part of the Gobi Desert is located in Gansu, as well as small parts of the Badain Jaran Desert and Tengger Desert. During his time in China, Hedin would meet the nationalist leader Chiang Kai-shek. His expedition would even behonoured by a Chinese postage stamp series. On returning to Europe Hedin published his findings, adopting a Turkic word "yardang" meaning "steep bank" to describe some of the most peculiar and spectacular rock formations he saw. The word is now commonly applied to express bedrock hills carved by wind and sand erosion into fantastic and unusual shapes. Yardangs can be found in most deserts around the world and have even been observed on Mars. The Chinese use a transliteration "yadan" to describe the phenomena.

Visiting Yadan

At the entrance to Yadan, there's a visitor centre, restaurant and museum of meagre interest. The restaurant also doubles as a guesthouse, with grubby rooms situated just off the main dining room where one can stay overnight. Showers, alas, are a luxury reserved for the staff only; fresh water is of a premium this far out in the desert.

There are regular bus tours through the park. But the best way to experience the desert would undoubtedly be to camp beneath the stars. However this remains a grey area, as the park administrators discourage visitors from camping in the park with lurid tales of

wolves and other potential predators. Sadly the majority of visitors will barely spend one hour here, alighting with their cameras for a brief stop on the Yumenguan tour from Dunhuang.

Yadan is a highlight of a visit to Dunhuang and if your budget stretches to this, it may be worth considering hiring a private car so that you can enjoy more time here. Inside the Yardang area there are jeeps for hire (from RMB300-1,000/hour with driver) that can cope with the desert terrain but stir up incredible dust clouds – make sure you don't get stuck behind one. *Entrance to the park costs RMB120/person, including a seat on a tour bus (RMB95/concessions.)*

4 Yangguan · Grape Valley

This excursion southwest through the desert takes in the one of the most enjoyable museums in China at the romantic Yangguan, site of another Han dynasty border gate, and offers an opportunity for bucolic relaxation in Yangguan's Grape Valley.

Yangguan – The Sun Pass (阳关 , Yángguān)

Located approximately 70km southwest of Dunhuang, Yangguan (The Sun Pass) was a customs checkpoint on the border of Han dynasty China. Constructed in the 1st century AD under Emperor Wu, Yangguan was a key site on the Silk Road overseeing trade and the exchange of goods and ideas with distant empires. Just like Yumenguang, Yangguan has been eulogised by poets from various dynasties who perceived a certain sombre romance at the thought of life on the very edge of civilisation. The Tang dynasty poet Wang Wei, for instance, penned the immortal lines in his poem Seeing Yuan Er off on a Mission to Anxi: "Let's finish another cup of wine, my dear sir, you'll have no chance to meet a friend beyond the Yang Pass."

Today, what remains of the old border checkpoint is little more than a hilltop ruin. But there's plenty more to experience at the affiliated Yangguan Scenic Area which includes a comprehensive museum and reconstructed fortress aimed at giving visitors an insight into life on the frontier two thousand years ago.

Yangguan Scenic Area Museum

The habit of reconstructing historical sites can disenchant some Western tourists who would rather see an authentic ruins than something built yesterday. But the eleven year-old Yangguan Scenic Area gives visitors a real sense of what the fortress might have been like in its heyday, replete with battlements and ancient armaments.

Entrance to the museum costs RMB60/person. By booking online you can get a discounted price of RMB45. There are no English guides.

On entering, the first thing visitors encounter is a mighty statue of the great Han dynasty explorer Zhang Qian who helped open-up the "Western Regions" through two epic crusades during the second century BC. Zhang Qian's accounts were some of the first reliable Chinese accounts of the lands beyond the Hexi Corridor, including detailed descriptions of ancient kingdoms occupying parts of modern-day Pakistan, Tajikistan and Xinjiang.

The affiliated museum tells the epic story of the Silk Road and is home to a kaleidoscope of artefacts unearthed around Yangguan, including ancient brick, chess pieces, bronze horse & cart ornamentation and pottery.

Beyond the museum is a gatehouse from which people would have entered and exited China in ancient times. Tourists can re-enact setting out on an epic voyage by dressing-up in dynastic robes (RMB20) and getting a bamboo passport stamped with the imperial seal which is marked with your name and the date you "departed" China. The ancient passport makes a great souvenir at RMB70.

Beyond the gate, chauffered donkey carts take vistors up the hill to the remains of a preserved Han fort (RMB10/person). From the base of the fort one can enjoy an unrivalled panorama of the desert, and imagine what it was like for ancient traders to set out on the danger-fraught Silk Road.

By Yu Xin,
(513-581)

On the long road from the Yang Pass,
Not one person returns.
Only the geese on the river,
fly south for the winter.

The Grape Valley of Yangguan (阳关葡萄谷 , Yángguān Pútáo Gǔ)

The area around Yangguan is a centre of the local grape and wine industry which has developed in the past thirty years. Grape Valley makes a pleasant place to visit for lunch and it is even possible to stay the night at a vineyard come guest house.

When establishing desert outposts, officials of the Chinese Empire had to consider one principle concern, namely, how to secure a reliable supply of fresh water. Therefore the site of the Yang Pass was chosen due to its proximity to a desert spring, which today waters the Grape Valley of Yangguan.

The Sogdians, an ancient people of Iranian descent who occupied an arid land in modern-day Tajikistan, first brought the technology of underground irrigation tunnels to China making life in a place with very little rainfall possible for Chinese on the frontier. Centuries later they would bring their appetite for sweet fruit as well.

The Chinese had known about grapes since Zhang Qian's expeditions and had grown them in small quantities. But the Sogdians fashion for making wine from grapes trickled down the Silk Road slowly and it was only by the Tang dynasty the Chinese were writing poetry dedicated to this intoxicating nectar (though it never supplanted rice or grain wine as the most popular tipple).

Appearing as if in defiance of the laws of nature, this predominately rural hamlet has tree lined streets and running streams of crystalline water. Heavy bunches of grapes hang from vines in the many vineyards packed into this tiny fertile enclave. And over the past decade a few entrepreneurial farmers have converted their homes into guesthouses and restaurants.

Where to Stay

There are six Peasant Family Guest Houses in Grape Valley. The largest and first to open was the Old Yangguan Farm Music guest house and restaurant, situated on Longlei Road in Yangguan Township, where one can dine in the vineyards on local favourites like Aubergine, Chilli, Tomato Noodles or Braised Mutton. The restaurant also hosts a mobile library.

Further down the road is Pan Family Grape Garden, a guesthouse / restaurant that has hosted leading government officials in the past. Five ensuite guest rooms in the vineyards behind the house offer visitors a unique locale to rest their heads after a bottle or two of Mogao Dry Red.

Grapes

A favourable environment of plenty of light, warmth and unpolluted water means that Yang Town grapes' have a mellow taste. Several different grapes are under cultivation in Dunhuang including Wuhebai, Manaizi and Purple Pearl.

Wines

Mogao Dry Red is a well known and rather palatable medium dry wine. Meanwhile the fruity and elegant Mogao Ice Wine is popular at state banquets. Both wines can be purchased at supermarkets as well as tourist sites around Dunhuang.

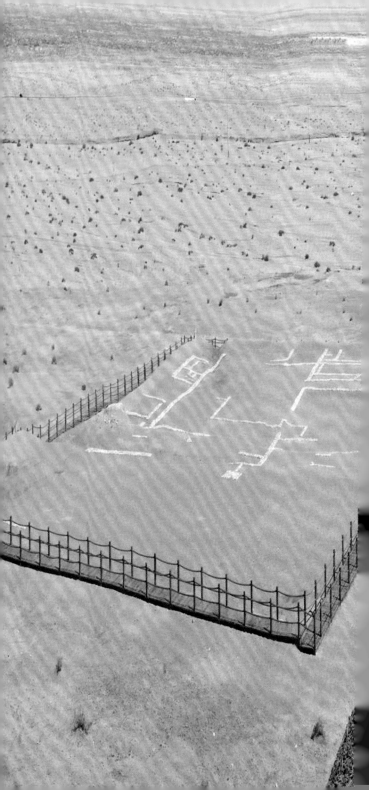

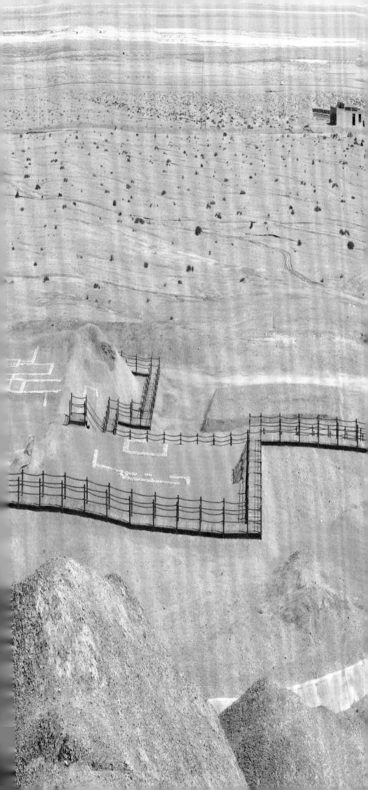

5 Xuanquanzhi Post Station · Suoyang Ruins · Yulin Caves

En route to the Buddhist caves site of Yulin, visitors will pass through some stunningly bleak desert scenery as well as a spattering of verdant oasis towns. About forty minutes along the road from Dunhuang is the site of a Han Dynasty post station. If the journey onto Yulin proves fatiguing, Suoyang (Tashi) is the principle stop-off point. It's essentially a grubby hamlet with a few small eateries. In the surrounding desert however are well-preserved ancient ruins.

Xuanquanzhi Post Station
(悬泉置 , Xuánquánzhí)

North of the Sanwei mountains, 4km from Dunhuang at the edge of the Gobi desert, is the archeological site of an important post station on the Han dynasty Silk Road. Built between 2BC and 2AD as the Han tightened their grip on the Hexi corridor, the Xuanquanzhi Post Station was key to Han control of the Silk Road in this region. The only such site of Han times to have been identified in modern times, this is a place to let one's imagination roam free to touch the past.

Visiting

Xuanquanzhi Post Station lies south of Highway S314 from Dunhuang towards Guazhou. The site was excavated between 1990 and 1992. As no public transport stops here and the turn-off is not signed, it is really essential to have a car with a local guide. Visitors must disembark by the main road and walk along a desert track towards the site. The 1.5km track peters out at a hut with a small exhibition about the excavated post station, which lies beyond. Although the site is supposedly open from 8am to 6pm, when we visited it was locked, but an attendant was persuaded to open up. There are plans to upgrade tourist infrastructure soon, with a proper road to be cut from the S314. No doubt this will mean the start of ticketed admission but for the moment entrance is free.

There is little to see at what is essentially an archeological site nestled serenely at the foot of a mountain. A raised wooden boardwalk laps a 50sqm area with labels indicating different areas of the post station including stables, a watchtower, a waste disposal area and an ancient toilet. Frequent helpful notice boards in Chinese and English offer informative tipbits about the workings of a Han dynasty post station.

Among the 17,650 relics dug up here was a wall epigraph from Emperor Ping of the Han dynasty which is one of the earliest known edicts on environmental protection. A still more important find were 450 fragments of hemp paper, of which 10 are the world's oldest known survivals of paper with writing on them. 35,000 mostly wood document slips were also dug up, many with inscriptions, and a wide variety of high quality silks, wooden combs and brushes and other everyday objects. Many of these artefacts are displayed at the Gansu Province Museum in Lanzhou where they provide visitors with a sense of life on the edge of empire in Han times.

Suoyang Ruins
(锁阳城 , Sǔoyáng Chéng)

Scattered evocatively across the Gobi desert are the ruins of the old Silk Road city of Suoyang, one of the largest and best preserved city ruins in Northwest China. Founded during the Western Han dynasty as Kugucheng, Suoyang really flourished during Tang times, when it acquired its current name. Unsurprisingly given its border location, the city had a strong military flavour, housing large camps of soldiers as well as the residences of military officials and their families.

Visiting

The unprepossessing small town of Suoyang (also known as Tashi) lies about halfway between Dunhuang and Yulin and makes a reasonable place to break the journey to Yulin and get something to eat. The ruins of the ancient city are in the desert to the east, about 30km south of the modern town of Guazhou on Highway S314. There is no public transport to the ruins and so it is necessary to hire a car. Suoyang could be visited as a dedicated day trip from Dunhuang or incorporated into a self-made itinerary including the Yulin caves and Xuanquanzhi Post Station.

The ancient city has two main sections. The first, known as the Outer Fort, covers an area of 800,000 sqm and is largely an extension of the city built during Tang times. The second, the Inner Fort, occupies a mere 28,000 sqm of which a large part was used as a horse breeding area by Chinese military forces. The Inner Fort was surrounded by 8m tall walls and on the northwest side of the city there stands a 18m high watchtower. There is also a well preserved tower of Tang construction.

The city's defense structures and irrigation system remain in impressive condition. Although most of the ruins are Tang, there is also a physical legacy of other eras, including more than 1000 small Yuan dynasty towers and a temple from the same period, located on the northeastern side of the city. *Entrance to the Suoyang Ruins is RMB10.*

Yulin Grottoes
(榆林窟, Yúlín Kū)

The site of the Yulin Grottoes is some 100km outside of Dunhuang, in Anxi County and is best reached via private hire car or tour bus. On the way you might even catch sight of a few wild camel herds. There are only 800 camels left in the wild making them a critically endangered species. *Entrance to the Yulin Caves costs 40 yuan for a tour of about eight caves (no English guides.)*

History

Situated on the banks of the crystalline Tashi River (also known as the Yulin River) as it flows through the stony valley of Mount Nanshan, the Yulin Grottoes comprise 43 decorated Buddhist caves. Colloquially referred to as the Ten Thousand Buddha Gorge, the grottos festooning the river walls are of various epochs: Four date to the Tang dynasty, eight date to the Five dynasties period, 13 date to Song dynasty, one to the period of Uyghur dominion, four are from the Western Xia dynasty and three are from the Yuan dynasty. The caves fell into misuse during the Ming dynasty but ten caves were rebuilt during the Qing dynasty, though the quality of painting and sculpture largely fails to live up to their ancient predecessors' work.

Artistic Legacy

Adorned with stunning sculptures and wall murals, the subject matter and means of expression in the caves have much in common with the Mogao Grottoes. The majority of the caves take the form of an entrance corridor, antechamber with a main chamber embedded deeper into the rock as the principle hall of interest. Some 42,000 sqm of wall painting and over 250 sculptures have survived into present day. The Yulin Grottoes, like other Buddhist caves in the region, are under the protection of the Dunhuang Academy.

Caves

Cave 3 *(Western Xia)*

Built during the Tangut dominated Western Xia era, this special prayer cave is from the eleventh century. Some believe the Western Xia Emperor was the cave's chief patron. The symmetrical designs exhibit heavy Tibetan influences. The murals are some of the most beautiful in Dunhuang, in particular a Han-style black ink painting of sacred Mount Emei enhanced by mineral colour pigment. There's also an early painting of Tang monk Xuanzang returning home to China. He has a halo, signifying he has become enlightened.

Cave 6 *(High Tang)*

Outside this cave we find tiger and dragon Arhats that were added in the late Qing dynasty. Inside there is a giant, 24.7 metre high Buddha statue. This is the third biggest Buddha in a Dunhuang grotto. The cave's patron Empress Wu Zetian claimed to be the future Buddha Maitreya, which this statue depicts. The cave took two generations approximately 30 years to build. Due to a flood in 1911 and dragon pillar was constructed in 1912 to protect the cave.

Cave 11 (Middle Qing)

This cave is known as the Dragon King Cave. It was constructed by Daoists to appease the Yulin River's propensity to flood. The statues depict deities of nature, including wind, spring, thunder and lightning. A gold coloured dragon king sits in the centre. The eight immortals, Daoist saints, are depicted on the ceiling. The cave also contains 18 Arhat statues that were retrieved from Cave 3 in 1989 and date back to the Western Xia.

Cave 12 (Five Dynasties)

The Cao family donors of this cave temple are depicted in traditional Han attire burning incense. Opposite we find their wives adorned in Tang chic with phoenix hairstyles and broad sleeved gowns. Birds and flowers surround them. The central statue is Qing but is of a famous Sui-Tang doctor named Cong Simiao. Medicine servants sculpted by Daoists attend him. The wall paintings are original tenth century murals.

Cave 13 (Five Dynasties)

In the 11th century when this cave was painted, the mineral pigment malachite green was particularly in vogue. Despite water erosion we can see beautiful water flowers on the ceiling ringed by a pattern based on the Chinese character 回 . The principle statue of the Buddha is of late Qing dynasty provenance and is thus not very aesthetically endearing. He is depicted with a deer, which signifies the first preaching.

Cave 14 (Song)

The 900 year old ceiling of this cave is the best-preserved in Yulin. There is a lotus flower in the centre, surrounded by the "hui" 回 design and strings of pearls, suggesting Persian influences. The eleventh century statue of Sakyamuni resembles a Chinese emperor. The proportions are excellent but the Qing dynasty repainting leaves much to be desired.

The Buddha is surround by six disciples of Qing dynasty provenance. A fire pattern halo is painted on the wall behind the statues.

Cave 15 (Middle Tang)
During the middle Tang, the Hexi corridor was occupied by Tibetans. In the inner corridor we see a Tibetan style heavenly king – a serious expression and slim body. Elegant Han paintings adjacent show the blend of cultures at this time. Nepal and Indian influences are also evident in this most cosmopolitan of caves. The main chamber was decorated in the eleventh century, which was painted over the original eighth century murals. The Bodhisattvas are grey, thin, androgynous and depicted without moustaches, which is consistent with the Tibetan style.

6 Dunhuang Town And Around

Dunhuang, one of four fabled frontier garrison towns, is today, a pleasant relatively modern prefecture level city, devoid of the pollution and congestion that tarnishes many Chinese cityscapes today.

A large part of the 2000 year old city is wedged between two waterways, the Dang River to the west and the Trunk Canal to the east. Tourists tend to gravitate towards the neighbourhood surrounding the Dunhuang Mosque where the Night Market and Snack Street offer a great area to unwind, shop for souvenirs and tuck into the local delicacies. The area is also festooned with Lanzhou Pulled Noodle restaurants should you be seeking a quick and hearty bite.

Dunhuang has all the amenities you'd expect in a relatively prosperous town including shopping centres, a sports stadium, hospitals, and post offices – should you wish to send a few postcards home. There are also plenty of small shops, hotels and and restaurants catering to visitors and locals alike. The municipal government is more or less in the centre of town should you need a place of reference, which is only a short walk from Dunhuang Museum.

The locals' preferred recreational area is around the Dang River, west of which many new housing estates have been constructed to cater for the growing number of urbanities. The tourist dollar has attracted developers here too. One of Dunhuang's largest hotels Grand Soluxe sits on the riverbank while the area is also alive with restaurants, retail outlets and places of relaxation.

Administered by the nearby city of Qiuqian, Dunhuang's population has swelled over the last decade from 180,000 at the turn of the millennium to 200,000 in 2014, due in

part to the development of tourism. Dunhuang is by no means big by Chinese standards and the city centre is easily negotiated on foot. The metropolitan area covers 6.47 square km and there are relatively few tall buildings. Like many modern Chinese cities, Dunhuang has been redeveloped since economic reforms in the 1980s. The city streets are flat and generally straight, following a grid pattern. Cycling is an ideal way to get around and experience the city but pay attention to the local driving etiquette.

Dunhuang Night Market
(敦煌夜市 , Dūnhuáng Yèshì)

This thriving commercial stretch in the predominately Muslim quarter of town is a must for souvenir hunters. Dunhuang's Night Market has its share of tourist tat stalls – postcards, novelty items and t-shirts produced in East Coast factories, abound. But this is a city built on cultural tourism, and furthermore it has long been a cultural crossroads, thus the market is great place to sift through traditionally Chinese products, as well as seemingly foreign articles.

The Dunhuang Art Silk Carpet shop located at number 63 of the commercial street embodies Dunhuang's uniquely cosmopolitan handicrafts. This store sells the kind of rugs and carpets most would associate with the Middle East. Yet Manager Sun insists Dunhuang has a long tradition of carpet making and the designs, though fused with Persian and Arabic influences, are definitely Chinese.

In the night market one can also find the fine silks synonymous with trade in this part of the world. Additionally jade, the Chinese enthusiasm for which opened the Silk Road in the first place, is also on sale, carved to form animals from the Chinese zodiac, regal ornaments or jewellry.

Dunhuang City Museum
(敦煌市博物馆 , Dūnhuáng Shì Bówùguǎn)

The City Museum opened in 2012 and while a work in progress appears to be well on its way to becoming a fitting showcase for Dunhuang's cultural heritage. From 1 May to 30 September the museum is open from Tuesday through Sunday and the opening hours are 8.30am – 6pm. From 1 Oct – 30 April the opening hours are 9am – 5.30pm. The museum has a roster of guides fluent in English and other major languages. Visitors enter through a small corridor which is currently bare walled except for outline sketches of what will eventually become simulacra of famous Mogao murals.

The first room contains an introduction to the history of Dunhuang's assimilation into the Han empire under the Han Wudi emperor, the epochal expeditions of Zhang Qian, and Ban Chao, and the opening up of the Silk Road. Perhaps the most compelling exhibits are everyday relics of Han times, well preserved by the dry climate and sand. Pairs of ancient socks and wool lined shoes poignantly evoke their ancient owners, as do wooden objects like chopsticks and combs.

The museum contains complete replicas of a few Mogao grottos including the famous (and usually off limits) High Tang Cave 45. There is also a reconstruction of a Tang dynasty tomb.

The history tour unfolds chronologically towards Dunhuang's Tang dynasty peak, with explanations about the increasingly sophisticated land cultivation that supported Dunhuang's emergence as an international trading centre. Relics from the Tang period include Go pieces, which were mass produced in the area for the royal court.

The museum mines detail of the Mogao murals such as the famous execution scene from Cave 45 for insights into social history. Several of the murals illuminate the improvement in women's status in the time of Tang Empress Wu Zetian, one of the most powerful women in Chinese history.

Dang River (党河 , Dǎng Hé)

Dunhuang's life-giving Dang River has been turned into something of an attraction in its own right. If you look closely, the real river gushes brown water parallel to the blue manmade waterway, where you can enjoy recreational actives like peddle-boating. At night the Dang comes alive with a water and light show, with dragon fountains belching plumes of illuminated water spray into the night air. It's impressive stuff considering how little rainfall Dunhuang gets. The river is also bordered by landscaped parks and exercise grounds. Locals hop across the river on a series of gimmicky bridges. One of the best places to enjoy the scene is a teahouse situated in one the faux Ming-style temples on the West bank of the river. The surrounding neighbourhood is flush with hotels, restaurants and shops.

Artists Village (敦煌艺术家村, Dūnhuáng Yìshùjiā Cūn)

In the dusty lanes of a nascent artists village several studios can be visited. Officials donated cheap land for the establishment of airy studios set in leafy grounds and inhabited by artists drawn here by Dunhuang's good light, cheap living and glorious artistic heritage. The studios are generally happy for visitors to drop by and no appointment is necessary. Several understandably concentrate on reproductions of the Mogao cave murals, a skilled practice through which artists come to an understanding of the achievement of their ancient predecessors. It makes for a relaxing diversion to tour the studios, which are located close to one another. If you are with a Chinese speaker then you can talk to the artists and their students (who come from all over China) about their work and their impressions of Dunhuang.

Lei Yin (Thunder) Temple
(雷音寺 , Léiyīn Sì)

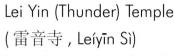

Located near the Mingsha dunes, the historic Lei Yin (Thunder) Temple is the only working temple with this name in Northwest China. The front courtyards are the older, dating back to the 1980s, while the back part is being reconstructed on the model of the monastery portrayed in the Tang dynasty Pure Land mural of Cave 172 in the Mogao caves.

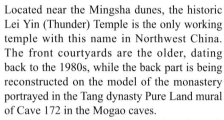

Visitors explore three courtyards each boasting a main hall and side buildings. The first courtyard's Hall of the King of Heaven hosts a jolly fat gold Maitreya Buddha. Garish coloured huge statues of the four big kings of heaven hulk in the side arches. The gate to the second courtyard, whose green tiled roof is appointed with eave decorations of dragons and small lions, leads to the Hall of Great Wisdom. Sakyamuni commands its centre and on his left and right are the Medicine Buddha and Amitabha. The north and south walls are embellished with copies of Mogao murals.

From the back of the second hall you emerge onto a Worship and Overview Platform, which is the best place to view the reconstructed Tang monastery. Simply magnificent, the Tang monastery must be one of the best reconstructed ancient building complexes in China. All buildings are wood, which looks splendid but is a fire risk necessitating strict regulations about incense burning.

The Bell Tower and the Drum Tower, summon monks to prayer in the morning and at night respectively. Framed by the two towers, the third palace at the back of the third courtyard is called the Palace of Light. In keeping with Tang architectural principles, no nails were used in its construction. The palace houses 24 gods to protect the Buddha.

About 30 monks work at the temple and 15 to 20 are in full time residence If you visit at the right time, it is possible to join the monks for free vegetarian food.

Entrance to the temple is free. Breakfast is served at 5.30am, lunch at 11.30am and dinner at 6pm.

Dunhuang Movie City
(敦 煌 电 影 城 , Dūnhuáng DiànyǐngChéng)

Dunhuang Movie City is located just 16km out of town, and while many tourist buses bolt this onto their Yumenguan itinerary, it may be more fun to visit independently. This citadel of kitsch was built in 1987 as a film set for a Japanese funded production. Since then it has hosted stars of the Chinese screen such as Jackie Chan.

Imposing but rather new looking grey city walls dangle with impressive siege weapons and are ringed by spikes, battering rams and projectiles. A wooden watchtower looms above the gates. The entrance fee is RMB40. There are no English speaking guides here but imaginations may be stimulated by a number of activities. Visitors can ride a steed in the horse yard, or for RMB50 trot around the whole city. Other available anachronisms include archery.

The 150,000 sqm city is laid out in different historical zones. The first, Dunhuang Street, resesembles an old style Dunhuang commercial street. There are shops and official's houses, and visitors can rent dynastic costumes to blend in with other tourists wandering the city like extras in a Zhang Yimou epic.

Next up is Gaochang Street, simulating an ancient city in Xinjiang. This area of dusty mud houses is popular for filming dramas of the Silk Road. For added authenticity the mud was imported.

The Tang dynasty zone boasts a bustling market and a calligraphy centre where the sign inscriptions that are such a feature of Movie City are made by Ren Wen Hui and her family. Ganzhou Street's parade of cigarette kiosks and drug store simulates the Gansu town of

Zhanghe. Another parade of mud houses, and courtyard houses with wooden roofs is in the style of Yingchuan in Ningxia.

The Song dynasty area is modelled on the ancient Chinese capital of Kaifeng. The highlight here is a Song style wine house where you can sit and drink Mogao dry red wine.

Practical Information

Accommodation

Your biggest choice is whether to base yourself downtown or at the Mingsha dunes. In the city you can pick from a range of moderately priced business hotels along with budget and higher end options. Out at the dunes, conditions are more bucolic, with Charley Johng's a popular backpacker stop. Many guesthouses offer meals and some will also organize a night under canvas in the desert. Meanwhile if you are visiting Yangguan you might want to consider overnighting in a vineyard.

Price for a standard double room in peak season :

¥   below RMB200
¥¥ RMB200-500
¥¥¥ RMB500+

Downtown

Dunhuang Hotel (敦煌宾馆)

151 Yangguan Middle Road, 阳关中路 151 号 ; tel. 973-8859128; ¥¥¥

Chinese Communist Party bosses reputedly favour this 32,000m landscaped four star hotel when they visit Dunhuang. The hotel's 500 beds include presidential rooms and deluxe suites. There are Chinese, Western and Japanese restauarants.

Dunhuang Five Ring Hotel (敦煌五环宾馆)

520 Mingshan North Road, 鸣山北路 520 号 ; tel. 937-8836574; ¥¥

This reasonably priced hotel, ten minute's walk from the Night Market, is also convenient for transport to major tourist sites in the Dunhuang area. The bus to Mogao stops 100m to the left of the hotel doors, while 100m to the right you can hop on a bus to Crescent Moon Lake. The hotel organises a special tourist bus service to Yadan.

Dunhuang Legend Hotel (敦煌飞天大酒店)

15 Mingshan North Road, 鸣山北路 15 号 ; 937-8853888; ¥¥¥

Rooms at this supposedly four star establishment peak at above RMB1500 in high season but at other times can be booked for far less. The amenities include a health club, a Chinese restaurant and a coffee shop, and English speaking staff.

Feitian Hotel (飞天酒店)

15 Mingshan North Road, 鸣山北路 15 号 ; tel. 937-8853999; ¥¥¥

Centrally located, this comfortable high class hotel boasts a large lobby with a wooden staircase and luxurious Mogao themed decorations. The hotel's superior amenities include KTV private rooms, a gym and massage centre.

Home Inn (如家酒店连锁)

Intersection of Mingshan Road and Ning Sai Road (opposite the old bus station), 鸣山路与宁塞路交叉口（原老汽车站对面）; tel. 937-8878-333; ¥¥

This branch of the popular Chinese mid-range hotel chain is conveniently located on Mingshan Road. On offer is solid comfort with reliable WiFi and hot water. Prices vary depending on season.

KuaileYizhang Youth Hostel (快乐驿站青年旅社)

Xiru Road 50m to west of Night Market, 西域路沙洲夜市南门向西 50 米 ; tel. 13830744331; ¥

A budget option close by the Commercial Street and popular with young Chinese travelers. Beds in an eight-person dorm cost as little as RMB30, while a family room is about RMB200 depending on season. The hostel organizes a range of activities

including camel hikes and bike rides, but language could be an issue for non-Chinese speakers.

Tianrun International Hotel (天润国际大酒店)

309, MingShan Road, 鸣山路 309 号 ; tel. 937-8818888; ¥¥

This standard business class joint sits in the heart of the tourist area at the intersection of Mingshan Road and Western Road. From here it is a five minute stroll to the Night Market and Dunhuang Snack Street. There are two buildings: the main hotel; with a business centre and a small shop; and a nearby annex.

Seven Days Inn (七天酒店)

323 Shazhou South Road, 沙洲南路 323 号 ; tel. 937-8608777; ¥¥

The cheerful yellow logo of this budget hotel chain is ubiquitous in many Chinese cities. Rooms usually cost around RMB200 a night, although they can be higher in peak season. For your money you get small but clean rooms with hot howers and free WiFi.

Mingsha Dunes

Charley Johng's Hostel (敦煌月泉山莊－青年旅舍)

Beside the Mingsha Dune, in the Crescent Moon Lake agricultural area (鸣沙山下，沙生植物园（月牙泉农家园内）; tel. 937-8833-039, email dhzhzh@163.com; contact Yang Xiaoyang(杨 小 艳 ,) mob. 13993733106; ¥-¥¥

Thanks to its foreigner savvy management and a location by the Minghsa dunes, Charley Johng's has become a popular hangout for hipsters. The rustic setup of rooms around an open courtyard makes this a relaxing spot to spend a few days. The hostel offers many services to enrich your stay, including camel treks, bike hire, luggage storage, ticket booking and laundry.

Charley Johng's also runs a smaller downtown hostel at 21 Mingshan Road where many of the same services are available as well as a 'western' breakfast (also available to non-residents.)

Dunhuang Hill Resort (敦煌山庄)

5 Shanzhou North Road, 沙洲北路 5 号 ; tel. 937-8882088; ¥¥¥

Consider this Hong Kong-invested tourist hotel as the luxury option for those wanting to stay near to the Mingsha dune and Cresent Moon spring. The hotel's 270 rooms make a stylish base for appreciating the desert landscape. Places to relax include a coffee shop and bars.

Yingyue Hill Resort (映月山庄)

West of the entrance to Mingsha Hill (鸣沙山月牙泉景区入口西侧); tel.937-8882-888; ¥¥

Among the cluster of guest houses and hostels dotted around the semi-agricultural land of the Mingsha Dune area, Yingyue stands out as being relatively clean, modern and quiet. However the prices here are also higher, comparable to mid-range hotels downtown.

Yadan

Yadan Restauarant and Guesthouse
(敦煌雅丹餐厅能住宿)

Beside the Yadan Museum at the entrance to the YadanGeopark (雅丹博物馆旁边); contact Tan Xiaowei (谭 小 伟), mob. 15097242566/13993733455; ¥¥

Five rooms are available here for tourists that want to overnight in the desert. The rooms, which can be reserved for about RMB280/night, each have two beds. Although the rooms are clean, they are basic with no Wi Fi or shower facilities.

Budgeting

Dunhuang is way cheaper than China's more developed cities such as Beijing and Shanghai but entry to the various ticketed sites, not to mention extracurricular activities like camel riding, can mount up. Bear in mind that the underdeveloped tourism infrastructure may leave you spending more than anticipated on private cars or taxis If you stay in a cheap guesthouse at the dunes, rely as much as possible on public transport and tourist buses and eat in local restaurants, then an average budget of RMB400/day should be sufficient. If you prefer to book a business class hotel and travel in style by private car then you could blow upwards of RMB1000/day. In the end it should be possible for those of all budgets to enjoy a rewarding trip. Guideline costs in Chinese Yuan (CNY) are as follows:

Main course at a budget/moderate restaurant: RMB30/RMB80
Double room in a budget/business class hotel: RMB120/RMB350
Taxi to/from Dunhuang airport/ Mogao Caves: RMB50/RMB40
Place in car tour to Yumenguan/Private car hire for one day: RMB400+
Admission to Mogao Caves and Digital Centre: RMB240

Chinese Festivals (2015, 2016, 2017)

Chinese New Year
(Feb 19, Feb 8, Jan 28)
Lantern Festival
(Feb 24, Feb 14, March 5)
Qing Ming
(Tomb Sweeping)
Festival
(April 5, April 5, April 4)
Dragon Boat Festival
(June 20, June 9, May 30)
Mid-Autumn Festival
(Sept 27, Sept 15, Oct 4)

Exchange Rates as of June 10, 2012

Australia AUD1 = CNY5.12
Canada CAD1 = CNY5.35
Euro zone EUR1 = CNY7.70
Hong Kong HKD1 = CNY0.80
Japan JPY1 = CNY0.05
New Zealand NZD = CNY4.83
Singapore SGD1 =CNY4.72
UK GBP1 = CNY9.72
US USD1 = CNY6.19

Food

Dunhuang cuisine is of the northwestern ilk synonymous with Xian. Noodles, not rice, are the dominant carbohydrate, while mutton and beef supersede pork and chicken as the principle meats in the region. Flavour tends towards the sour and spicy, with dishes soaked in vinegar and chilli peppers.

As one might expect, Gansu's principal fast-food export Lanzhou Beef Pulled Noodles can be found everywhere: Just look out for white heat-tempered Hui Chinese hands stretching sticky dough and then boiling it at the eatery's door. All the Hui restaurants serve halal certified produce.

Although braised meat features, prominently in Dunhuang fare, vegetarians need not fear going hungry thanks to local specialties like Qielaxi. Vegetarian fare can also be shared in Buddhist temples like Leiyin Temple by the dunes. Some famous local dishes include:

Dunhuang Yellow Noodles
黄面

Depictions of people making yellow noodles appear on Mogao murals, proving their long popularity. The heavy dough is pulled into thread-like noodles which are boiled in water and eaten at room temperature. They are typically served with other dishes. This Dunhuang staple supposedly resembles threads of gold – which may be fanciful, but they are undeniably tasty.

Braised Donkey Meat
(烤驴肉)

Gansu is the gourmet capital of donkey cuisine. One local saying has it like this, 'In Heaven there is dragon meat, and on Earth there is donkey meat.' Donkey meat is supposedly sweeter and more tender than horse meat and is low in fat and high in protein. The meat can be sampled as donkey kebabs on the street, or as donkey burgers, but why not go for the full monty of donkey with yellow noodles.

Braised Lamb Cakes
胡羊焖饼

This delicacy made from boiled mutton and thin floury cakes is a local snack in demand since Sui and Tang times.

Dunhuang Dumplings
敦煌水饺

Dumplings, known as shuijiao, are recorded in Dunhuang books dating back to the Wei and Jin dynasties. Popular local fillings include lamb and fennel and mushroom and turnip.

Qielaxi 茄辣西

This classic Dunhuang vegetarian dish is essentially tomatoes, peppers and aubergine poured over a hearty bowl of noodles – be warned, portions are not small!

Getting Around

Tourist Buses

Hopping on one of the popular tourist buses is an inexpensive and efficient way to take in the region's major sights. Tickets can be bought at hotels around Dunhuang and at the Charley Johng's café on Mingshan Road. The buses also pick up from downtown hotels. There are two major tourist bus itineraries, each with two daily departures from downtown Duhuang.

The first route takes in the following sights: Yadan National Geopark – Han Great Wall – Yumenguan – Western Caves. The first departures is at 7.30am and returns to Dunhuang at 5pm and costs RMB76. The second departures, which leaves at 2.00pm and gets you back at 11.30pm, costs an additional RMB10 but includes sunset at the epic Yadan National Geopark.

The second route includes all of the above sights but adds on Yangguan. The morning departure leaves at 6.30pm and costs RMB100. To experience sunset at Yadan then take the 10am bus which costs RMB120.

Bike Rental

Cycling is a great option for getting around town as Dunhuang is flat and dry. The going rate is RMB/10 hour or RMB50/day and bikes are available from a spattering of shops in the downtown area, including Time To Go (TT GO) on Western Road. However, many of Dunhuang's most notable sites are located far from the city district in the desert, so unless you're an experienced cyclist with appetite for endurance and hardship, you'd best opt for motorised transport.

Taxis

Taxis are cheap and fairly plentiful. The flag drop is RMB5. Outside of the city centre, drivers will often prefer to negotiate a fare rather than use the metre. Other than the lexicon of lucre, little English is spoken by drivers.

Public Bus

Dunhuang is a relatively small city with the town centre negotiable on foot. There are three main local bus routes. The only inner-city busing you'll likely want to do is from the two major hotspots of Minsha Hill and downtown Dunhuang (stops include the Dunhuang Hotel.) Bus #3. Price RMB1. Every 20 minutes.

Private Car Hire

Due to the distance between Dunhuang's major points of interest and the sanitary, hop-on-hop-off nature of tourist buses, it is well worth considering hiring a car. A chauffeur driven saloon, people carrier or SUV will give you the freedom to enjoy

Dunhuang at your own pace. There are also certain sights too far away to be included on bus tours.

One agency offering places on private car tours is Shared Car Hire (拼车旅游聚划算); tel. 13519072355/ 13830706676.

The following routes are available:
1. Crescent Moon Lake – Mogao Caves. RMB150/car.
2. Dunhuang Movie City – Western 1000 Buddha Caves –Yangguan–Yumenguan–Han Great Wall –Yadan sunset.RMB500/car.
3. Yumenguan– Han Great Wall –Yadan RMB400/car.
4. Jiayuguan Pass.RMB900/car.
5. Yulin Caves –Suoyang Ruins. RMB650/car.

It is also possible to arrange your own itinerary with a driver for about RMB400-500 per day depending on the itinerary and the size of the vehicle you wish to hire.

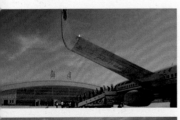

Getting There

Plane

There are no direct international routes to Dunhuang and so visitors will likely change plane at either Beijing, Shanghai or Xian. A direct flight from Dunhuang to Xian takes about two hours, and three hours from Dunhuang to Beijing. There are also services from Dunhuang to Hangzhou, Nanjing, Chengdu, Dalian and the northwest cities of Lanzhou and Urumqi.

Daily services from Dunhuang are as follows:
• Beijing - dep. 11:20, 15:40, 21:30
• Lanzhou - dep. 11:45, 11:55, 20:15
• Xian - dep. 10:10, 11:55, 15:40
• Chengdu - dep. 11:45
• Urumqi – dep. 14:25, 16:35
• Shanghai - dep. 15:40
• Dalian - dep. 15:40
• Hangzhou – dep. 17:25
• Nanjing – dep. 20:15

Dunhuang Airport
(敦煌机场)

Information: 937-8866133;
Flight booking: 937-8822389
http://www.dhjichang.com

Dunhuang airport (IATA: DNH) is located 13km east of downtown. The taxi fare to downtown from the stand outside the airport, is RMB50

These taxis do not usually run on the clock. Hourly shuttle buses also depart and some of the better hotels will pickup. Alternatively, stroll ten minutes to the new train station and catch a bus into the city.

Train

A train approach to Dunhuang across the desert is a romantic choice. Many rail passengers will embark at Xian, home of the terracotta warriors. Be warned though that even on a "fast" train this is a twenty-hour hour journey.

Train services from Dunhuang are as follows.

• Lanzhou - #Y668, dep. 17:57 arr. 09:50
• Lanzhou - #K9668, dep. 19:22 arr. 09:36
• Xian - #K592, dep. 09:32, arr. 09:22
• Jiuquan - #7528, dep. 16:08, arr. 21:51

Dunhuang Rail Station (敦煌火车站)

Tel.937-5959562/ 937-5955229;
http://www.dhhuochezhan.com

The relatively new Dunhuang train station is about 12km outside the town to the northeast. Tickets can be bought at ticket agents and hotels downtown.

LiuYuan Rail Station (火车站)

Liuyuan Town, Guazhou County,
瓜州县,柳园镇
Tel. 902—7130222;

Dunhuang train station is pretty quiet as most trains stop at Liuyuan (柳园), a couple of hours away from the city. From Liuyuan there are trains to a far wider range of destinations, including Beijing, Shanghai, Guangzhou, Chengdu and Urumqi. A taxi from Liuyuan to Dunhuang costs about RMB240.

Bus

Bus travel is a way to really get under the skin of China's vast northwest. There are two daily departures to Lanzhou, at 11:00 and 15:30 and the journey takes about 17-24 hours. Other popular destinations include Jiuquan, a prefecture level city in northwest Gansu that is one stopping off point for Jiayuguan, the location of the Jiayu pass of the Great Wall. There are at least ten daily services and the journey takes 4-8 hours. Meanwhile there is one daily departure to Urumqi at 19:00.

Dunhuang Bus Station (敦煌汽车站)

Sanwei Road (near Jiangrong Market),
三危路（建荣市场附近）;
Tel.937-8822174/937-8822129
http://public.dha.ac.cn/content.aspx?id=843704266483

Local Products

A colourful range of local agricultural and handicraft products are available at markets and shops around the town and make good souvenirs and curiosities.

Agricultural products

A number of shops along Western Road sell dried fruits such as grapes and dates and other produce such as wine and tea. However the same products can often be bought cheaper in local supermarkets.

Grapes: Dunhuang yields upwards of 3800 tons of grapes a year. The grapes are sweet and delicious. They can also be bought at vineries around Yangguan.

Dried apricots: Another famed local product, apricots are resistant to the cold and grow well in the dry climate of Dunhuang.

Dates: Grown on Ming Mountain in Dunhuang, the local dates are large, at about 40-50g, and the meat is tasty and sweet .

Jujubes: In Dunuhuang, jujubes are placed in a jar, pickled in white spirits and eaten in autum and winter.

Elm flowers: Dunhuang people are acccustomed to eating elm flowers, which are in blossom every spring. The locals pick the flowers, wash them clean, then mix them with flour and steam them.

Xiangshui Pear 香水梨

Xiangshui pears are a traditional Dunhuang delicacy that have been cultivated for a long time. The pears are stored until winter when the frozen fruit turns black.When thawed out to eat, the soft and juicy pears have a delicious sweet and sour taste.

Craft products

A good place to look for local artistic creations is Commercial Street which during the daytime hosts a crafts market. Here, as well as in permanent stores along the street, you will find celebrated Dunhuang products like Dunhuang Luminous Cups, carved gourds, strange stones, decorated fans and cuddly camels.

Dunhuang Luminous Cups: The cups are first mentioned in Records of Ten Famous Places All Over The World written by Dong Fangshuo during the Western Han dynasty. Tang dynasty poet Wang Han also eulogised 'grape wine with luminous cup.' The cups are made from high quality ink jade from the Qilian mountains.

Mural and statue copies: These can be purchased at bookstores along Commercial Street, markets around town, at the Mogao Caves bookshop, or at studios in the artists' village. Artists such as Zhang Daqian, Hang Shuhong and Dong Xiwen have all worked in Dunhuang creating the reproduction murals.

Strange Stones: Fascination with strangely and suggestively shaped stones is a keystone of Chinese culture that goes back at least to the Song dynasty. Dunhuang strange stones are rocks that are natural without any carvings at all. The stones are treasured for their visual beauty and analogic suggestiveness.

Treasures of the Study: A number of antique and bookstores along the night market street sell calligraphies, paintings, the 'four treasures of the study' (writing brush, ink, inkstone and paper), jade ware, jewelry, porcelain, copper ware, root carvings, old coins, and stamps.

Nightlife

The Night Market is the first port of call for more foreign visitors and gets lively with outdoor tables, free flowing beer and occasional karaoke act. There is also a more local scene of cafes and restaurants along the Dang River.

Dunhuang Book Bar
(敦煌市淘趣书吧)

95 Dunhuang Commercial Street (商业街 95 号); tel. 937 8889508; contact Mr Ma (马 先 生), mob. 18919462202;
One of Dunhuang's coolest hangouts on the Commercial Street, the Book Bar offers two floors of laid back sophistication. Sofas, shelves of books and a cool terrace on the third floor overlook the Commercial Street action.

Massage

Higher end hotels like the Dunhuang Hotel offer massage. One more economical option for a foot or body massage is Jinxiu Foot Massage (金秀足道) at 210 Western Road next to the Mogao Hotel. Prices start from RMB80 for one hour.

Song and Dance

Every night at the Dunhuang theatre there are song and dance performances based on scenes portrayed on the walls of the Mogao caves. A number of spectacular shows with acrobatic antics and ever changing backdrops have been devised, including Tales of the Silk Road, Dunhuang Dream, Dunhuang Goddess, and Thousand Hand Guanyin Boddhisatva Dance.

Dunhuang Theatre
(敦煌大剧院)

777 Yangguan Middle Road, 阳关中路 777 号 , tel. 937-8832959.
Nightly performances: 20:30-22:00
(May 1 – Oct 20 only.)
Ticket prices: RMB200/person.

Outdoor Activities

Dunhuang offers visitors the chance to experience a range of outdoor activities including camel riding, offroading and sliding on sand. Many are available at the Mingsha dunes (see page 78.) Other exotic diversions you might try in Dunhuang include archery and paragliding.

Boating: Boats, pedillos and water bicycles can be rented on the downtown stretch of the Dang river. A 15 minute peddle boat ride is RMB15/10 (adults/children,) or RMB45/boat. Motor boats are RMB50/person for half an hour, with a RMB100 deposit.

Camel Rides: These are the favoured way to tour the Mingsha dune and Crescent Moon Lake: the circuit costs RMB100, not including an optiona ticket for sand sliding. Remember to hold onto your ticket!

Cosplay: Your hankering to dress up as a Han emperor or Tang courtesan can be satisfied at the Dunhang Movie City. Costumes can also be worn at the Yangguan museum (from RMB20.)

Helicopter: Rides are available at the Mingsha dunes. Prices start from RMB280/person for a short hop, through to RMB3780 for a tour encompassing the Mogao caves and Sanwei mountain.

Jeeps: Can be hired (with driver) in the Yadan Geopark. The cost is RMB400-600 depending on the route.

Light Plane: Can also be rented at Mingsha dunes. Prices range from RMB33,000 for dedicated use to just RMB1760 for a two or three person plane.

Off road: At Mingsha, you can race around the dunes in a quad bike from RMB300/person.

Sand sliding: Two types of mats are available for your descent from the top of the Mingsha dune. Bamboo (RMB15) and tyres (RMB25).

Restaurants and Cafes

The most vibrant nighttime eating area is on Commercial Street, adjoining Dunhuang Night Market Square. This outdoor barbeque emporium resonates to the song of serenading musicians while the air chokes with exotic spices. Despite being a Muslim area, beer is served in large canisters placed on tables. Yellow River Beer is preferable to Dunhuang's flat and insipid local brew.

The downtown area is full of restaurants ranging from Lanzhou Pulled Noodle joints to yellow noodle and donkey meat specialists. A good place to sample esoteric local cuisine is the Dunhuang Snacks Street (敦 煌 特 色 小 吃 街 ,) a strip of specialist kiosks whose boards advertise appetizing sounding fare like Cooked and Chopped Entrails.

Mutton Braised Cake (胡羊焖饼)

On the Dunhuang Snacks Street (鸣 山 北路敦煌特色小吃街内)

This kiosk at the north end of the Dunhuang Snacks Street serves a range of local delights including vegetarian dumplings, lamb noodles, tofu and beansprout and qielaxi (tomato and eggplant.)

Daji Donkey Meat and Yellow Noodles (达记酱驴肉黄面馆)

Just west of the Tianrun International Hotel (天润国际大酒店西侧); contact Da Chunpeng (达春鹏), mob. 13893763456.

This highly rated but moderately priced local institution is a good place to try classic Dunhuang dishes like yellow noodles and donkey meat. The restaurant's traditional décor features murals of Asparas. Other tasty dishes - many for under RMB30 - include spicy tofu noodles.

Golden Bay Farm (金水湾农家乐)

Yangjia Bridge (first unit), 杨家桥一组; tel. 13993722749

Golden Bay's specialty is agricultural produce grown on the attached farm. The delicious vegetable dishes sourced from fresh farm produce include spicy eggplant and tomato, fried bitter melon. Donkey meat is also available for incalcitrant meat eaters!

Hui Wei Zhai (回味斋)

1st Floor, 12 Mingshan Road (beside the Mogao Hotel), 鸣山路12号 (莫高宾馆一楼); tel. 937-8842112

Close to the southern entrance to the Dunhuang Snacks Street, this well established restaurant offers a range of local fare including dumplings. The restaurant has an English speaking waitress, and Wi Fi, and will accept large parties.

IllyCafé (意利咖啡)

2, Mo Yuan Street, Dunhuang Commercial Street, just off the Dunhuang Night Market Square 墨缘街2号, (商业街南门, 敦煌夜市广场中间); tel. 937-8858916, 133-0937-3881;

This café at the heart of the Commercial Street is a popular hangout of foreign travelers. Beer costs RMB10-15 and you can also binge on coffee and ice cream.

Knight Coffee (黑骑士)

First Floor, Real Eust Company Building, Xinjian Road (opposite the south end of Commercial Street), 新建路, 房产公司综合楼一楼 (商业街斜对面)

A convenient refueling stop for coffee, wifi and pastries close to the Commercial Street and Night Market.

Oasis Homemade Ice Cream (路过饮品店)

61 Dunhuang Commercial Street (just off the Night Market Square), 商业街61号; tel. 13830706352; Contact: Yu Hai Tao 余海涛, good English; email: oasisicecream@163.com,

This little café serves delicious home made ice, yoghurts and milkshakes. Try the peanut butter ice cream. Beer is also available.

Shirley's Café (敦煌风味餐厅)

MIngshan Road (opposite Feitian Hotel), 鸣山路飞天宾馆对面; Tel. 937 8837078; ;contact Zhang Zhijun, mob. 18919420078

Shirleys on Mingshan Road one block from the Tianrun Hotel is an oasis of western run café culture: the place to come for your western breakfast of yoghurt and museli, banana milkshakes and pancakes.

Shunzhang Yellow Noodles Restaurant (顺张黄面馆)

Building One, BinheShijieJiayuan, Jinshan Road (near Jinshan Hotel), 金山路, 滨河世纪家园 1 号楼 (近金山宾馆) ; 937 8824910

Another premium destination to enjoy the famous yellow noodles is Shunzhang which claims a history going back to the Qing dyasty.

Yang Family Restaurant (杨家庄)

Yangjia Bridge, opposite the village cultural centre (杨家桥, 乡文化站对面); tel 937 8833467; contact Yang Xin (杨鑫), mob. 13993703287

Yang Family Restaurant specializes in home cooking with the fresh produce making this a good place to try local vegetarian hits such as garlic fried potato and eggs with wood ear mushroom.

Yi Xian Wan Muslim Restaurant (伊祥苑清真餐厅)

2 Xinjian Road, 新建路 2 号 ; tel. 937 8825763

Despite its name this popular establishment offers not just Hui style muslim fare but dishes from all around China.

Yangguan Farm Restaurant (阳关农家乐)

Longle Village, Yangguan Town (阳关 镇 龙 勒 村); tel. 937-8601159; contact DuanHaihong (段海宏), mob. 13893762588

This restaurant among the vineyards offers a bucolic setting for a long lunch of local fare washed down by Mogao Dry Red Wine. Visitors may stay here and the restaurant also houses a local library. Opening times: 8:30-12:00, 14:30-18:00,19:30-21:30.

Shops

The tourist hub around Xinjiang Road and Mingshan Road has a cluster of convenience stores and supermarkets. You will find banks with ATMs, including a branch of the China Construction Bank at 551 Mingshan Road. The adjacent travel agencies cater for local tour groups. Next door to the Guangyuan Hotel, at 619 Mingshan Road, there is a pharmacy. The Runwan Jia Shenghuo Supermarket on Western Road is a good place to stock up on snacks for desert sojourns. It is open from 8.30am to 11pm (10pm in winter.) The Dunhuang Bookstore on Western Road stocks a few English books about Mogao. TT Go sportswear shop is a good option for bike hire and you can also buy a camping stove and outdoors clothes.

China Carved Gourd Art
(中国微雕葫芦艺术)

54 Commercial Street, 商业步行街 54 号 ; tel. 13209406630

A place to encounter the art of gourd carving.

Dunhuang Specialty Store
(敦煌敦盛特产店)

First Floor, Real-Estate Building, Xinjian Road (opposite south entrance of the Commercial Street); tel. 937 8888889

This is a good shop to explore a diverse range of Dunhuang craft products, from agricultural products like dried grapes and dates to wood sculptures, stone paintings and glowing cups.

Junwei Camping Gear
(军威户外休闲装备)

7 Mingshan Road (opposite the Mogao Hotel), 鸣山路, 7 号, 粮食局家属楼下 (莫高宾馆对面) .

Shop here for sleeping bags, water proof mattress, cooking stuff and telescopes – everything you might need for that night in the desert.

TTGO Bike (自行车专卖店)

First Floor Rea-Estate Company Building, Xinjian Road (opposite the south end of the Commercial Street).

This is a convenient place to hire a bike; RMB5/hr or RMB50/day. The shop also sells bike accessories and maintenance equipment.

Sheng Yu Zhu (声雨竹)

Lingyun Plaza, Mingshan Road opposite the Tianrun hotel. 凌云商厦 ; tel. 937 8815886

Taiwanese fashion.

Ya Shi Zhai (雅石斋)

49 Commercial Street, 商业街 49 号 ; tel. 13809373755; Contact Xia Jianhua.

This shop on the Commercial Street sells books about Dunhuang as well as local craft products such as Dunhuang Strange Stones.

Useful Numbers

Police	110
Directory Enquiries	114
Ambulance	120
Fire Service	119
Weather Forecast	12121
Air Ticketing	2581
Railway Information	2585
China International Travel Service	86-10-65222991
Dunhuang Tourist Authority	400-006-5761

Dunhuang Tourist Authority

Tianmao Travel Mart

 Dunhuang Public
WeChat Account

 Dunhuang Tourism
Weibo Account

Useful Websites

CNVOL.com (China train schedules in English) http://www.cnvol.com/	
Ctrip.com International (Largest website for China hotels and flights) http://english.ctrip.com/	
China Tourist Maps http://www.chinatouristmaps.com/	
Dunhuang Academy (English website) http://en.dha.ac.cn/	
Travel China Guide(Train and flight schedules.).) http://www.travelchinaguide.com	
China International Travel Service http://www.cits.net/	
International Dunhuang Project http://idp.bl.uk/	

Useful Phrases

Hello	nihao (nee how)
Goodbye	zaijian (dzayjenn)
Please	qing (cheeng)
Do you speak English?	ni hui yingwen ma? (nee whey Eeng-win ma?)
I'm sorry	duibuqi (dway-boo-chee)
Yes	shi (shir)
No	bu (boo)
Excuse me	qing wen (cheeng wen)
How much is that?	duoshaoqian? (daw-show-chyen?)
How do I get to…?	dao…zenmezou? (dow…dzummadzow?)

INDEX